MECHANICAL TIN TOYS
IN COLOUR

# Mechanical Tin Toys in Colour

*ARNO WELTENS*

BLANDFORD PRESS
POOLE          DORSET

Originally published in the Netherlands by Uitgeverij Kosmos bv 1977
Original Dutch title: Mechanischblikken speelgoed
First published in England 1977
by Blandford Press Ltd.
Link House, West Street,
Poole, Dorset BH15 1LL

World copyright © 1977
Uitgeverij Kosmos bv, Amsterdam.
English edition copyright © 1977
Blandford Press Ltd.

ISBN 0 7137 0848 4

Text printed and books bound in Great Britain by
Richard Clay (Chaucer Press) Ltd., Bungay, Suffolk

# Contents

Dedicated to my wife Bea and our cat Vladimir

# *Introduction*

When I started collecting tin-plate toys some years ago I had no idea that I would one day write a book about the subject. But, like every hobby, as soon as you go into it seriously a new world is at your feet.

As a child I knew only the dying days of tin-plate toys, but on seeing a bright fire-engine with its battery lighting, water-tank, extending ladder and clockwork mechanism I was reminded of a present I had had for my sixth birthday. Once again the charm and ingenuity of these toys impressed themselves upon me. Generally these cheap mass-produced toys had a limited life in the hands of a child, but they stand the test of time compared with the plastic goods sold today which are often irreparably broken after one blow or fall.

Not only their durability, but the variety of form and different methods of propulsion have made these mechanical tin-plate toys such favourable collectors' items. There are some toys for which a collector is willing to pay a great deal of money!

In order to value a certain item it is important to know the manufacturer or trademark and the period in which it was produced. This information is essential for repair or restoration. For this purpose too, old manufacturers' and department stores' catalogues are useful; several have recently been reprinted. Nevertheless intensive inquiries are sometimes demanded at libraries, exhibitions and of other collectors before you can discover where and when a specific toy was manufactured.

It has not been my intention to write the 'complete' book on the subject, but I hope I have been able to give some insight into the fascinating world of mechanical tin-plate toys.

I am very grateful to all those who have helped me in compiling this book.

*Arnhem, Spring 1977*                                    *Arno Weltens*

# History in a Nutshell

As early as 1660 a group of toy soldiers were made by special request for the Dauphin of France. They were designed by a well-known French architect, Sebastian de Vauban; the clockwork was made by Gottfried Hautsch and his father, who were Nuremberg blacksmiths. (Gottfried Hautsch who died in 1703 was famous for the tin soldiers he made.) Using silver as their material, they worked for four years on this project producing over a hundred soldiers which could really march and shoot. Unfortunately this unique piece of work has not been preserved for posterity.

King Louis XIV also had a unique coach and horses, specially made for him by the famous François Camus. It showed a lady sitting inside the coach, with a coachman and footmen sitting on the box. When the coachman gave a signal with his whip the coach moved off, and as soon as it stopped, the footmen opened the door and the lady stepped out. However, it is not known what mechanism was used by Camus.

There is a popular story that one day Napoleon bought hundreds of penny toys to be given away by his wife, the Empress Josephine, for the children of widows of soldiers killed during battle.

Queen Victoria also possessed some famous toys. Pieces such

as these were only made for Royalty and it took months, even years, to manufacture them. Jacques de Vancauson, a Frenchman by birth, born in Grenoble, devoted himself to the manufacture of mechanical toys. In 1738 he introduced his first mechanized toy, a 1·65 m (66 in) tall Satyr, playing the flute. Three years later it was followed by a mechanical drummer, and a gilt bronze duck, which could eat, drink, quack and flap its wings. Père Cruchet, also a well-known name in this period, made several mechanical toys. He was taken prisoner at the Battle of Trafalgar, and in 1815 settled in London. His mechanisms were similar to the ones Vancauson made, but a little simpler.

The year of 1815 is a notable date for the toy industry, because that was when the technique of printing forms in metal was discovered. According to a thesis by Otto Senft ('*Die Metallspiel-waren und der Spielwarenhandel von Nürnberg und Fürth*'), the technique was passed on in 1822 to Vienna by German labourers. A few years later it was used in Nuremberg, but unfortunately the precise date of its use is unknown.

The town of Nuremberg is also famous for the development of the pocket-watch, thimble, clarinet, fire-engine and the wheel-chair. In the Joh. Karl Lenchs sales catalogue of 1826 not only are wooden, alabaster, and pewter toys shown, but also a few examples of early tin-plate toys. The world-famous catalogue of Hieronimus Bestellmeier, however, is the best example. At the International Exhibition of 1851 in London, tin-plate toys from Nuremberg were shown for the first time. At that time only two manufacturers of tin-plate toys were registered in Nuremberg. Ten years later there were 241 small factories employing around 360 labourers.

These manufacturers pursued a steady course. When the idea of a new toy was born, a sketch and final drawing were made, followed by a model made out of wood. From this model a mould was formed in the foundry. For every single part of the toy, a mould was needed. The prototype was tested and any necessary corrections made; when everything was ready the production finally got under way. In the workshops tinsmiths, using the special presses at their disposal, pressed and cut the plate into the desired form. The parts were then passed on to the painting section where female workers plunged them into lacquer and put them into a drying-kiln. Details such as facial expressions were painted on with a brush. The clockwork mechanisms were assembled, the parts soldered together and then packed.

This method was particularly used by French toy manufacturers. The slot and tab method was mainly used by other countries. Later toy manufacturers used a lithographic way of decorating the tin-plate before stamping.

In France and Germany there were people working part-time in their homes. These labourers, living in stinking hovels, earned their daily bread by working very hard. They collected all types of scrap metal, storing their finds in their homes, and as these included tin cans, which sometimes contained remnants of food, the smell was quite appalling. They recycled this material into new tin-plate toys. This kind of work was also done by French prisoners in the Santé Prison in Paris.

The American toy manufacturers used thicker coats of paint. Their models were not as perfectly finished or detailed as those of their European competitors, but the use of bright colours (hand-painted) compensated for this, and in this way the American toy manufacturers developed their own style. The creations of Althof, Bergmann & Co., George W. Brown and Edward Ives are among the best examples. Althof, Bergmann & Co. was founded in 1856 by the three Bergmann brothers. During 1870–85 they manufactured several lovely clockwork toys including an American speciality, the hoop toy. Fastened to the inside of a hoop, was a clockwork figure which, when wound

*Section through a toy rabbit (Martin), 1890*

up, propelled the hoop along the ground.

George W. Brown and Edward Ives started respectively in 1856 and 1868. The George Brown Company carried for a couple of years a beautiful collection of hand-painted locomotives, coaches, horse-trams and so on. At first Brown's fellow countryman, Ives, manufactured tin figures which were powered by heat (for instance a candle). In 1870 Ives moved to Bridgeport and from that time developed a collection of mechanical tin-plate toys. The first item he made was a racing boat which operated in the water as well as on the ground. The clockwork used came from the 'New Haven Clock' Company.

Elastic bands were also used as simple mechanisms (see cutaway illustration above) even before they were used in model planes. Nearly all toys before 1900 were powered by a simple flywheel mechanism. About 1880 Ernst Paul Lehmann, who was one of the most popular and famous German manufacturers, introduced the coil-spring clockwork.

Unfortunately there was no talk of any standardization in clockworks, because every toy had to fulfil special demands. Special gears were applied to lengthen the winding-up mechanism of the clockwork. Some firms specialized in manufacturing clockwork mechanisms. Mechanisms were highly ingenious and

*Horsewoman (flywheel driven)*

reverse engineering was often used (for example, a cart pushing a horse). Although these toys were made out of tin-plate, they were quite solid, in spite of the indentation and rusting of the material.

Many toys worked on the gravity or inertia principle. In this method a heavy flywheel was used, thus creating so-called friction power. In Europe they applied this form of power from *c.* 1880 to 1910. In the United States, however, they liked the robust form better and, because it was also cheaper, they stuck to it longer. By pulling a string or moving a switch they could give the flywheel its initial velocity (see illustration above). These gaily coloured Victorian toys were a feast for the eyes. Still, they were rarely more than 20 cm (7 in) tall and had no musical box like 'automata'. We can distinguish two groups of metal toys:

(*a*) non-mechanical tin-plate toys (drums, sand-castle moulds, buckets, etc.).

(*b*) mechanical tin-plate toys (toys driven by any mechanism). This group also included humming-tops and construction kits, such as Meccano.

One of the first well-known German manufacturers was Theodore Märklin. He started with his wife in 1859 with the production of children's cooking equipment at Göppingen. In 1866 Theodore died, due to an accident, and his wife Karoline had the heavy task of continuing on her own. Possibly she was the first woman commercial toy traveller in Germany and Switzerland. However, she was not totally successful. In 1888 her sons, Eugen, Wilhelm and Karl, had to carry on without the necessary finances as the Gebrüder Märklin. In 1863 Ignaz and Adolf Bing started a wholesale business in toys and household goods at Nuremberg. After a couple of years they started their own production. The Bing firm grew rapidly and became the leading manufacturer in this field. Their toy assortment consisted of trains (clockwork, steam and electric), railway accessories, ships, cars and steam-engine accessories. In spite of annual sales of about 27 million DM in 1928, Stephen Bing could not prevent the approaching depression. The Wall Street crash of 1929 dealt the death blow to the Bing concern.

In 1869 Jules Steiner from Paris introduced some velocipedes (bicycles). The most important French toy manufacturer, however, was Fernand Martin who owned a factory on the outskirts of Paris, which turned out some 800,000 mechanical tinplate toys between 1878 and 1912. Then the firm was taken over by Bonnet & Cie. His creations were sold by street pedlars or in the cheap stores in Paris. In the Conservatiore des Arts et Métiers in Paris, there is a selection of his work including a clown sketching, a swimming fish, a magic ball with a hidden acrobat inside it and a billiard table with players.

The Decamps family had a small factory in Paris at the same time. Their finish is similar to that of Martin. Péan Frères, a Frenchman too, also earned a certain measure of fame for his toys.

In 1877 the German firm S. Günthermann started manufacturing mechanical toy jockeys. In 1880 the firm Britain and Sons made some remarkable pieces. Only nine examples have survived, but they give us a good example of the design and construction of British clockwork toys. In 1881 Ernst Paul Lehmann started in Brandenburg (Prussia); his trademark was formed by the interlaced initials EPL. 90 per cent of his products were exported to other countries. Lehmann manufactured toys to match the way of life in other countries: the English 'Hansom Cab', the Japanese rickshaw 'Masyama', the American rodeo cowboy 'Broncho' and the Dutch miller 'Gustav'. He also developed the coil-spring clockwork in the form of a piece of piano string revolving round a tin cylinder with cogwheels fixed at each end. After his death, Lehmann's cousin, Johann Richter, took over the business. After the Second World War the firm moved to Nuremberg. They had to start from the beginning, for they had left everything behind in Brandenburg.

In 1882 Georg Adam Mangold started the production of mechanical tin-plate toys. He started with a small collection of mechanical animals. After 1890 the German manufacturers changed to the use of pre-printed tin-plate as basic material. It was the start of mass-production and the end of hand-made toys.

From that time all German toys carried the letters D.R.G.M., an abbreviation for 'Deutsches Reichs Gebrauchs Muster'. Permission was required if it concerned an improvement or addition to a toy for which a patent had already been granted.

D.R.P. was an abbreviation of 'Deutsches Reichs Patent', sometimes with the addition ang. for 'angemeldet' meaning 'applied'. The letters U.S.P. stood for the United States Patent, usually with a patent-number.

When someone took out a patent, it existed for a period of fifteen years and during this period the toy was protected against counterfeiting. A certain amount of money had to be paid for the patent. Some toy manufacturers became involved in a lawsuit on account of these patents, one of whom, Ernst Lehmann, was much in favour of them. Patents in other countries were required in the same way. Sometimes the inscription Ges. Gesch. (Gesetzlich Geschützt) or Musterschutz eigentr. was on the German toys. On the French toys the abbreviation 'Breveté S.G.D.G.' (Breveté sans garantie du Gouvernement) was printed. An abbreviation 'Sté'. referred to the firm or maker. From 1898 all tin-plate toys were labelled.

Trademarks were introduced earlier, because of the registration in several countries. In 1875 the Trademarks Registration Act came into force in England and in 1887 this Act was tightened up, so that counterfeiting or copying a registered trademark carried a sentence of two years imprisonment. 'Unis France' as an addition to a French trademark meant 'Union National Inter-Syndicale France'. The word dep. on German toys was the abbreviation of 'deponiert' meaning 'deposited' and was especially used in the surroundings of Nuremberg in Germany, where many small factories were started.

By 1900 Nuremberg and the neighbouring village of Fürth had sixty-five toy factories manufacturing metal toys. A total of 1,120 people worked in these factories, 661 of whom were women. Half of these people worked in four big firms in Nuremberg. The Germans could sell their toys more cheaply because of government support. Special concessions for rail and sea transport, subsidies, etc. made it very hard for other countries to compete with them.

In 1901 Frank Hornby took out a patent on the well-known Meccano system which he had originally made for his own children; until 1907 it was sold under the name of 'Mechanics made easy'. In 1905 Walther Stock founded a toy firm in Solingen. In 1906 Arnold from Nuremberg invented a novelty: the first tin-plate toys with built-in flint. In 1910 the English firm Lines Brothers was formed. The firm took over many others in the course of years and changed their trademark into Tri-ang Toys.

The Nuremberg firm Schuco introduced tin-plate toys, covered with velvet, in 1920. Birds and animals, such as bears, monkeys and rabbits were especially chosen as subjects; covering these toys in soft materials was probably for psychological reasons. A few years later Schuco succeeded in manufacturing the coachwork of cars in one piece. In 1929 they had a real hit: the world-famous peck-peck bird. Tens of thousands were sold over the years.

In 1930 Blomer & Schüler started (after originally making clockworks) with a small series of mechanical tin-plate toys. In 1932 Köhler followed the example of Blomer & Schüler.

Gradually the subjects produced became more interesting; it goes without saying that there was a huge range of cars, planes, trains, boats, etc. Some remarkable events, however, were also chosen as subjects, e.g. The South Pole Expedition of Amundsen in 1912 (Lehmann 'Ampoll'), the Boxer Rebellion in Peking (Lehmann 'Der bestrafte Boxer'), the Zeppelin (Lehmann, Distler), Lindbergh's Transatlantic Flight (Bing). Comic figures like Mickey Mouse, Pinocchio, Felix the Cat and Bonzo were also produced by other manufacturers. Warships, bombers, guns, armed and Red Cross trains were particularly popular during the war years.

In 1934 Philipp Ullmann founded the firm Mettoy in Northampton. In 1936 Fleischmann took over the Georg Staudt business. Just before the Second World War the German Johann Höfler established a small factory in Fürth.

Naturally the toy manufacturers had to work during both World Wars for their respective countries. They were forced by necessity into making weapons. Thus on 21 August 1944 a German order was issued strongly forbidding the production of any toys. The only exception made was in the manufacture of playing-cards for the soldiers.

Only a short while after the Second World War, Horn and

**Motor Lorry with Tip-Up Body.** Can be tipped as illustration. Superior quality and finish; strong clockwork movement, rubber tyres, front axle adjustable to allow either straight or circular run. 11¾ in. long, 3½ in. wide .. **5/11** Post 4d.

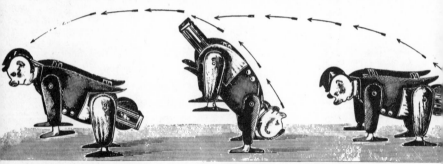

**Spring Heeled Jack.** Operated by momentum of heavy fly-wheel. Smart toy and quite original Price **2/11** Postage 4d.

**Mechanical Duck.** To run on the ground. Propelled by momentum of flywheel. Cannot get out of order. Splendid value .. .. **6d.** Post 3d.

0 Gauge. **Clockwork Train.** As illustrated. Consisting of Locomotive with strong clockwork patent regulator, with brake to be worked from rail or from the cab; tender and two passenger cars japanned and lettered in the exact colours of respective railway companies, with oval set of 6 rails including brake rail (4 curved and 2 short straight rails). Length of complete train 18¾ in.
Price .. **1/11** Postage 4d.

*Toys advertised in Gamage's catalogue, 1913*

18

## Clockwork Seaplane.

Special strong clockwork.
$4\frac{1}{2}$ in. high, $9\frac{3}{4}$ in. long, $11\frac{1}{2}$ in. wide.
Price **2/11**    Postage 4d.

## Mechanical Railway Porter.

An exceedingly clever Toy, with most lifelike movement. The man bends his knees and walks by mechanism contained in his body. Price **1/3** post 3d.

**Clockwork Swimming Lady** (as illustration). This is one of the most realistic Swimming Toys imaginable, it represents a girl in silk costume swimming the breast stroke, and propelled solely by the action of the legs and arms. Does not easily get out of order.

Price .. .. .. **6/11**    Post 3d.

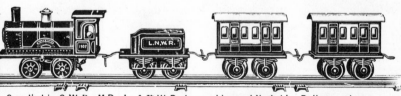

Supplied in G.W.R., M.R., L. & N.W.R., Lancashire and Yorkshire Railway colours.

Riemer initiated the rebuilding of German toy manufacture. By order of the Allied Forces all German tin-plate toys had to be marked 'made in U.S. Zone Germany'. This law was cancelled in the summer of 1948 when Germany got its own government back, although a few manufacturers maintained this addition for a couple of years. In future all German toys were marked, 'made in Western Germany', having only been marked 'made in Germany' before the Second World War. The German remnants which were spared in the war were sold in the 'Exchange Stores' of the American Army.

The export to America gathered impetus again because of the efforts of Louis Marx. At the end of 1945 he was sent ahead by the American toy federation to make inquiries about the situation in Germany.

Great difficulties faced toy manufacturers all over the world, the great lack of tin-plate, the basic material, being one of the problems. Others needed great effort to regain their properties and many factories and machines had been destroyed.

The situation in Germany was different, many small manufacturers had had to close down. The reason, perhaps, for the closures was the fact that before 1939 the wholesale selling outlet was in Jewish hands; thus after the war many contacts were lost. This led to selling problems, although many manufacturers persisted, and succeeded in establishing their own sales departments. Before the Second World War, foreign wholesale dealers visited Leipzig Fair which was held twice a year. Commission-agents showed their goods in assorted collections. On returning to their own countries the wholesalers displayed their selection to buyers, forwarding their orders on to Germany in time to meet the Christmas demand.

*Mechanical toys can be placed in the following categories:*
    (*a*) toy animals and figures

(b) humming-tops
(c) trains, tramways and cablecars
(d) boats, ships and submarines
(e) aeroplanes, zeppelins and bombers
(f) cars, motor-trucks, buses and fire-engines
(g) guns, tanks and armed vehicles
(h) bicycles and motor-bikes
(i) roundabouts and steam-engine accessories
(j) construction kits

## Toy animals and figures

Naturally all the European toy manufacturers who started their production after 1900, made a collection of mechanical animals first of all. By preference they chose a winged animal such as a duck, goose, chicken, turkey, peacock, butterfly or beetle because it was easier to imitate the wingbeat. They also used eccentric wheels to give these animals their staggered movement.

Dogs and cats were also favourite subjects. The dog was always chasing someone, whilst the cat was catching mice. There was a good range of the more exotic creatures such as ostriches, crocodiles or zebras, which were usually shown pulling a cart driven by a clown or another figure. Thus in making these toy

*Small bird (Mangold), c. 1930*
*The motion of the wheels worked the*
*bellows, enabling the bird to whistle.*

'Fix-Fax' no. 140 (Einfalt), c. 1930

animals, manufacturers were also contributing towards the education of children. The climbing monkey was on the market in many versions (Lehmann, 'Einfalt'): the American firm of Louis Marx had a climbing sailor version. The juggling or musical clown was also a favourite object.

*Humming-tops*
This sort of top was derived from the wooden whipping-top, which was popular in Germany. It was one of the first industrial applications of tin pressing; the shape of the top and bottom was pulled out of one piece of metal. Sometimes it went wrong, witnessed by the fact of the folds in the metal. You set the humming-top going by pushing a spiral wire up and down with a metal or wooden handle. The whistling or the music of the humming-top came from the vibration of metal strips in the bottom, and was also caused by the rotation, and the holes in the top. The illustration on the top, sometimes in relief nearly always showed children playing; adults were seldom represented. During the thirties Lehmann manufactured a mechanical hand-painted top, called 'Rollmops' no. 764. Inside the top was

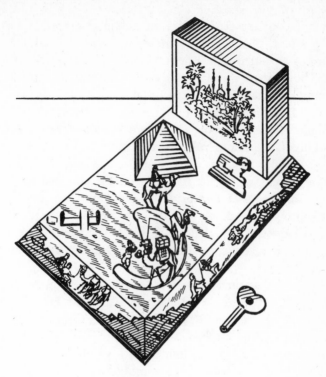

*Caravan scene set in Sahara (Mangold), c. 1930*

a mechanism with an eccentric weight so the top gave a drunken impression whilst in motion (see illustration page 128). The first models were hand-painted; later specimens were lithographically decorated. Well-known German manufacturers in this field were Bolz, Fuchs, Nüsslein and Rohrseitz.

*Trains, tramways and cablecars*
One of the first known trains with clockwork was 'the Rotary Railway Express'. A small green locomotive, with tender and

two Liverpool first-class carriages, it had tin-plate floors, soldered into position. The clockwork motor was also soldered into the centre of a painted lead weight and a wire arm, 45 cm (18 in) long, drew the train around in a circle. The key, which was cast in brass, was shaped like a serpent. The train sold in 1850 for 3 shillings including a box. In the period between 1850 and 1870 in France the firm Radiquet & Massiot started at the Boulevard Des Filles Du Calvaire in Paris.

The German firm of Mattheus Hess, was one of the first to produce trains without mechanism on the continent. At that period all manufacturers used the coil-spring and clockwork mechanisms first developed by the clockmaking industry. Special clockwork mechanism factories were opened to cope with this new demand, for example Bühler and Weiss in Nuremberg.

At about that time trains were also being manufactured in America by George W. Brown & Co. and Edward Ives. George Brown started in 1856 in Forestville, Connecticut, with the production of mechanical tin-plate toys. In 1868 Edward Ives started in Plymouth, Connecticut, with his brother-in-law Blakeslee. Two years later they moved to a new factory in Bridgeport, Connecticut, and clockwork trains (without rails) were added to the collection. Edward's son, Harry, joined the firm and after his father's death in 1918 took over the management of the firm. The name of Ives was never found on the toy itself or even on the packing, only the initials.

Characteristics of the early toy trains were the four spoked wheels and the engine with the tall, narrow chimney. In this age of steam many trains had built-in steam engines. The American Eugene Beggs from Paterson, New Jersey, was famous in this field about 1870. Between 1870 and 1890 cast iron was extensively used in the United States. Cast-iron toys were moulded in temporary sand moulds and grey iron was used as the raw

*Wind up 'Whistler' locomotive (Ives), c. 1880*

material. Sometimes small parts of brass–copper, lead or other materials were added. Cast-iron was used for the wheels too. Famous names in this field were the Hubley Manufacturing Company from Lancaster, J. & E. Stevens from Cromwell and the previously mentioned Edward Ives.

Despite American production many trains were still imported from Europe. There is quite a difference between the American trains and the imported ones. Only the imported ones carried Roman numerals on the carriages. With a sharp eye towards the American market, locomotives were produced with bells, cow catchers and headlights.

It is thought that the German Ernst Plank manufactured the first electric train. An article in the 1882 edition of '*Die Illustrierte Zeitung für Blechwarenindustrie*', was dedicated to this subject, but unfortunately no pictures of his novelty were illustrated. However, it showed how fast the toy industry

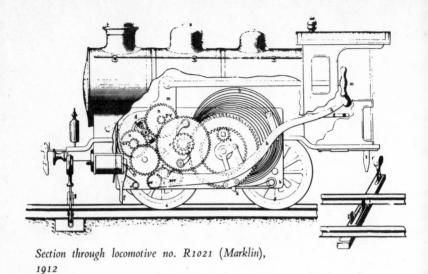

*Section through locomotive no. R1021 (Marklin),
1912*

caught on to new technical developments. Three years earlier,
Siemens had introduced the first electric locomotive.

The wet cells that drove the toy trains were very fragile and
short lived. The first electric train known, was introduced by
George Carette in 1893, followed by a copy by Carlisle & Finch,
Cincinnati, Ohio, in 1897. These trains were ahead of their time,
and not until 1910, when domestic electricity became common-
place, did they become very popular, although playing with
these early trains was a little dangerous. The trains either had to
be connected directly on to the household supply by means of a
special lamp, or run from an accumulator. Fortunately a couple
of years later with the new A/C household electricity supply
this problem was solved.

From 1860 until 1914 the German trains dominated the whole
toy market. Karl Bub started in 1851, Märklin in 1859 at
Göppingen, the Bing brothers in 1863 at Nuremberg, Ernst
Plank in 1866 and George Carette (originally a Frenchman) in
1886.

In 1891 Märklin was the first manufacturer who introduced train sets with a clockwork train on a figure-of-eight track. It caused a sensation at the Leipzig Spring Fair. It was also Märklin, who first introduced the numerical system of gauges, namely: 35 mm = gauge 0, 48 mm = gauge 1, 54 mm = gauge 2, 75 mm = gauge 3.

The export of Märklin articles went mainly to France, England and America. Gauge 3 was only briefly used by Märklin. Guage 0 and 1 were also used by Carette, Ives, JEP, Bassett-Lowke and even Bing. However, Bing and Carette used gauge 3 for 67 mm and that is why it was only an attempt at standardization. The first train-models were hand-painted and were sometimes trademarked. Later the models were lithographically decorated.

About 1905 Karl Bub started producing clockwork trains; he had been making tin-plate toys with and without clockwork for about fifty years. George Carette moved to Nuremberg in 1880 because of the low wages paid in Germany and the professional skill of the workers. At first he was a supplier for the Bing firm.

Most of the German trains were attractive in design, but were not very well copied. The Märklin models were an exception, offering to the public scale-model trains. Also a complete range of accessories such as stations, platforms, signals, tunnels,

*Railway tunnel no. 1441/3 (Schönner), 1905*

27

*Pulley wagon (wind-up type) no. 10/9204 (Bing),*
*1925*

bridges, switches, etc. were readily available to the enthusiast by leading manufacturers. In the beginning the points, signals and barriers were worked by air pressure.

The advent of the electric train, however, did not mean the end of the clockwork version. When the Paris Metro was opened in 1900, no time was lost in producing underground trains decorated with the coat of arms of Paris. Underground entrances were also available, the so called 'bouches du metro'. At the same time in Germany the monorail was very topical; in 1900 Bing had already manufactured a fantasy version of The Barnen–Elberfeld–Vohwinkel line, with a clockwork mechanism.

Märklin and Bing were the only manufacturers who produced clockwork tramways. All the others used electric trams with overhead wires. The current came from the midrail. It was insulated with rubber, but accidents still happened when the long couplings between the carriages hit the imperfectly insulated rail. The International Exhibition of 1900 in Paris was very important for the meeting which took place between Stephan Bing and the young Wenman Bassett-Lowke. This led to the production of well-known British locomotives in Germany and was the beginning of co-operation between the two firms. During the First World War this was severed.

Bing, who by preference made train sets in the popular price range, had the monopoly in this area. In 1911 Carette introduced a clockwork rack and pinion railway. In 1905 the Englishman Frank Hornby made his first clockwork train. His models were well detailed and the graduation scale perfect. Hornby trains became very popular, especially after 1917, offering a large assortment. In 1932 Hornby invented the first automatic coupling.

In 1910 Josef Kraus in Nuremberg began the production of clockwork trains, followed later by electric ones. Towards the end of the First World War some armoured train sets were available.

In the early thirties a rail zeppelin was offered by Bing as well as by Märklin; a clockwork or an electric 18 volt version in gauge 0 and 1 was available. The real rail zeppelin, a creation of Franz Kruckenberg, became the predecessor of the Japanese Tokaidoline and the French aerotrain. It had an inbuilt B.M.W. plane motor with a propeller at the back for propulsion. The metal frame was draped with insulated material and fire-proof canvas whilst the front of the train had a thin tin coating. This train broke the world speed record in 1930 and travelled at 230 kilometres an hour.

Johann Distler and Kindler & Briel were best known for their train accessories. In America the leading manufacturers of model trains were Lionel, American Flyer, New York Central Lines and Hafner.

*Boats, ships and submarines*
These toys were driven by clockwork, steam or electricity. Many were models of warships taken from the Spanish-American or the Russian-Japanese War. In Germany, Bing, Märklin and Carette were the leading manufacturers in this field. Their all-metal ships were strong, well finished and remarkably detailed. By removing the superstructure, which lifted off like a lid, it was possible to see the engine-room. As this was not a watertight lid,

however, many of the ships sank. Märklin ships, easily recognizable by their heavy beams, which sat low in the water, gave added stability and buoyancy. The Bing models, on the other hand, were slimmer and the decoration kept to a minimum. They used the same model for several versions. The small boats and ships had a clockwork mechanism, the bigger models a steam-engine or an electric motor. Some ships had little wheels, so the child could pull them along. One of the most amusing boats was the clockwork rowing boat (see illustration on page 49). In 1869 the American, Ives, made a very fine example. This model is now on show in the Bethnel Green Museum of Childhood, London. Many German ships were exported and given an English, American or French name.

The French made the most attractive specimens. Around 1890 Arnaud was recognized as one of the finest producers of boats, with hulls made of zinc, painted in black or dark green and finished with brasswork in the superstructure and fittings.

From 1914, because of the increasing motor power, ships

*Section through a steamship (flywheel driven)*

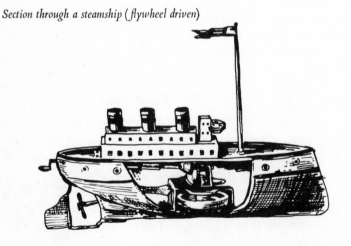

were given more funnels. Very popular was the so-called 'pock-pock' boat, a motorless craft driven by hot air.

All warships carried guns of one sort or another, including some which could be loaded with gunpowder; a few warships could fire their guns automatically. Next to the warships the most popular toys made were passenger, racing and tug boats. Submarines in several lengths were the follow-up, having a clockwork motor or a steam engine or were powered by battery. The French clockwork submarine shown on page 111 had an air tank under a screw top. Water entered through the exhaust, filling the tank and causing the submarine to submerge partially. It did not go under entirely, for the submarine had air tanks built in at the front and the back. The lacquer or finish was of a high quality to counteract rust. The screw top enabled the water to be poured out afterwards.

An improvement on later submarines was the addition of diving fins on the stern. When plastic came into fashion, toy boats and ships were the first objects on the assembly line.

*Aeroplanes, zeppelins and bombers*
Having seen the airship of Count Zeppelin (first flight in 1900) the German manufacturers introduced the toy zeppelin. In 1906 Lehmann introduced an attractive zeppelin made in tin-plate and celluloid. In 1919 Märklin also brought out two clockwork zeppelins.

Famous pilots like Blériot and the Wright Brothers made toy planes popular. At the end of the First World War the first bombers (biplanes) made their appearance. Although there was not a large choice of toy aeroplanes, everything changed after the famous solo flight of Charles A. Lindbergh across the Atlantic in 1927. Some of these models were attached by a string to a stick and flew round in circles, some also performed aerobatics. (See illustration of clockwork model made by

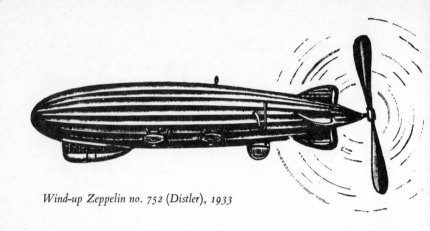

*Wind-up Zeppelin no. 752 (Distler), 1933*

Günthermann on page 55.) The autogyro, a predecessor of the helicopter, is shown on page 96. In 1930 the American firm Marx manufactured a clockwork plane with a parachute. The parachute was folded into the cockpit and, as soon as the propeller hit something, shot high in the sky, unfolded and returned to the ground. In 1936 Fleischmann offered a hydroplane which could fly tied to a cord or float on the surface of the water. After the Second World War the Spanish firm Payà manufactured a similar toy (see illustration on page 52). Some well-known manufacturers of planes were Günthermann, Tipp, Lehmann (especially zeppelins), I.N.G.A.P. and Payà.

*Cars, motor trucks, buses and fire-engines*
Perhaps through lack of interest in the real automobile, the toy car did not enjoy popularity. Toy manufacturers did not foresee the profitable future ahead. In the catalogue of a leading Parisian department store in 1902, only three toy cars are listed. Only two of the 170 pages in the catalogue of George Carette were devoted to cars. It is amazing that so many have stood the test of time. Perhaps parents were the reason behind this. It often happened that a toy car (or a train) were reserved for the

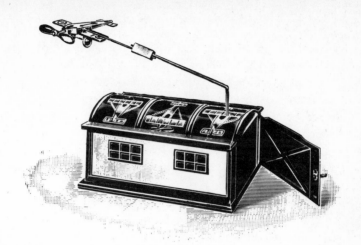

*Aeroplane with hangar no. 98a (Georg Fischer), c. 1930*

master of the house. Not only private cars, but also trucks, buses, racing-cars, fire-engines, etc. were sold. The more expensive cars even had passengers and the most elaborate had a cloth or a leather folding top, doors that could open, rubber tyres and a steering wheel that actually steered the front wheels. The most well-known means of propulsion were clockwork, friction, steam, dry battery or accumulator. Some car models had a small brake at the side (see illustration on page 102). In an old American toy magazine of 1914 electric cars were offered!

Probably the first race-track was available in two sizes. The tin-plate racing-cars with drivers had rubber tyres and ran on a circular race-track. A middle rail was the supply wire for the current and a drag-anchor under the car did the rest. The largest exporter was Germany, represented by firms like Bing, Carette, Hess, Günthermann, Lehmann, Märklin, Tipp and Stock. The Hess models were easily recognizable because of the starting-handle, with which you wound up the friction mechanism.

Most of the models were supplied to the export market with

colourful advertisements on them in the language of the countries to which they were going. This enabled the firms to make different versions from the one model. Some German firms sometimes exported the clockwork mechanisms themselves to other countries. The French produced only a limited range which were therefore of a better form and quality. Also the French firms, JEP, FV, C.I.J., Citroën and CR, preferred to use a thicker sheet metal and solder the parts together, where their German colleagues used the more popular slot and tab method. Thus, although the French models were more durable and attractive with their hand-painted exteriors, they were unable to compete with the more economical mass-production methods of their German competitors.

American manufacturers like Structo, Freeport and Wilkins Toy Co. (later taken over by Kinsbury) made their cars of cast iron, often unpainted. They also used their favourite friction power. Fire-engines with extending ladders had a special attraction for children. In 1914 the German firm, Ernst Plank, put an amphibian car on the market, which was followed in 1922 by a Lehmann version. In 1934 Schreyer & Co., Nuremberg, succeeded in making the first streamlined toy car together with

*Fire engine with watercannon no. 73 (Georg Fischer), c. 1930*

**New Model Open Touring Car.** Torpedo body.
Superior quality, best hand-painted, strong clockwork movement, nicely regulated rubber tyres, correct pattern seat with brake, f ont axle adjusted for straight or circle run. 9½ in. long, 3⅞ in. wide. Price **5/11** Postage 4d.

*Advertisement from Gamage's catalogue, 1913*

stamped coach-work. Even the headlamps were built-in, although at that time it was impossible for the car industry to do so on real cars; the headlamps were still assembled on the wings. Schuco had yet another novelty – the first mystery action toy car. It operated by means of a wheel, and it was impossible for the car to run off the table. As soon as the front wheels crossed the edge of the table, the fifth wheel came into operation returning the car on to the table.

In England only a few companies were active in the field of toy cars. Good models were offered by Bassett-Lowke, Burnett, Lines Brothers, Meccano and Wells. From 1948 until 1953 Mettoy manufactured some remarkable racing-cars with and without drivers.

In Spain the collection of firms like Payà and Rico consisted, for the greater part, of all sorts of vehicles in which there were some interesting model cars.

In Italy, Cardini, I.N.G.A.P., Metalograph and Omas, were

the leading toy firms in this field. They were stimulated by the big success of the renowned brands like Alfa Romeo and Fiat.

After the Second World War the model cars were typically American. German firms, like Arnold, Mangold, Schreyer & Co. also manufactured a collection which was probably connected with the many American military bases in Germany.

*Guns, tanks and armed vehicles*
There has always been a great interest in military toys and not only in wartime. To complete the collection of tin, pewter or lead soldiers there was a large selection of toy guns. Many of them could be loaded with wooden bullets, peas or pellets. As soon as the English used a tank in the First World War a toy version in camouflage-colours appeared on the market. Some special model tanks could run upside down. They had no gun turret, but the guns were mounted on the sides, so that when such a caterpillar-track vehicle met an obstacle steep enough, it crawled up, then flipped over and drove off. In 1934 Märklin introduced an armoured car, no. 1108 G., to complete the subjects in his range of car construction kits. During the era of military indoctrination of German youth before the Second World

*Field-gun no. 8042*
*(Märklin), 1929*

*Tank no. 22 (Georg Fischer), c. 1930*

War, great emphasis was placed on toy tanks, troop carriers and all types of military vehicles. Leading producers in this field were Tipp, Lineol and Hausser. In 1935 Karl Bub manufactured a gun construction kit, no. 921; India rubber shells as ammunition completed this adjustable gun. For the export market the colours and uniforms were adjusted to meet the requirements of other countries.

*Bicycles and motor-bikes*
At the end of the last century children played with clockwork bikes or tricycles ridden by dolls with porcelain heads or by tin figures. The thirties saw the arrival of the motor-bike and the three-wheeled carrier cycle (see illustration on page 67). Some motor-bikes had passengers on the pillion, or seated in the side-car. Around 1935 Einfalt introduced a novelty motor-bike which automatically righted itself when it fell on its side (see example of later model on page 73). Tipp, Kienberger, Arnold and Kellermann were the leading German manufacturers in this field. The great popularity of the scooter during the late forties and fifties, also provided manufacturers with a new subject to copy.

*Road-maker no. 925 (Doll), c. 1930*

### Roundabouts and steam-engine accessories

Roundabouts, with spindle movement (hand driven), spiral driven or battery driven, were mainly made by toy manufacturers who also offered steam-engines in various sizes. Clockwork roundabouts with small aeroplanes or zeppelins were sold by, among others, Althof, Bergmann, Blomer & Schüler, Krauss and Staudt. Steam-engines depicted many trades, among them the blacksmith, woodcutter, tailor, cobbler, butcher, scissors- or organ grinder. Also water- and windmills were favourite subjects; small fountains were also beautifully made, although zinc and brass was used in place of tin. The best-known firms in this field were Falk, Bing, Doll, Schönner, Plank and Märklin.

### Construction kits

Possibly the American firm Structo was one of the very first to manufacture a car construction kit. In the Sears, Roebuck & Co. catalogue of 1919 they offered a sheet-iron clockwork sports car. All the metal parts, including a clockwork motor, were neatly arranged in a cardboard box with a handbook. Price: $5.98. In 1936 Meccano offered its first car construction kit; it consisted of a chassis with three interchangeable bodies. This gave the builder the choice of two types of sports car or a tourer. The second set which offered larger models was available in several colour combinations. As a completing item, Meccano also offered a garage in which two cars could be parked. In France these models were produced by a subsidiary of the Meccano Co.

In 1932 the German firm Markes began the production of an aeroplane model series, nos. 104/106/108, followed by some model car construction kits with a clockwork motor. In 1933 Märklin launched his first car construction kit (see illustration on

*Dredging machine with waterwheel no. 270 (Falk)*

*Blacksmith no. 720 (Doll), c. 1930*

page 94). The main box for the chassis and clockwork motor could be completed by a choice of three coachwork boxes, namely no. 1103 ST for a streamlined car, no. 1104 P for a Pullmann-Limousine and no. 1105 L for a truck version. In 1934 a racing-car and an armoured-car version completed their collection. The coachwork for an oil tanker (Standard Oil) was the last addition in 1937. These models were sold until *c.* 1942. After the Second World War only the streamlined car, truck and racing-car were maintained and they remained in the Märklin catalogues until 1953. In 1937 Märklin had introduced a Junker plane kit which included a clockwork motor (see illustration on page 95). A handy illustrated guide book made it easy to assemble. These model planes were not reintroduced after the war.

In 1948 the Spanish firm Payà introduced the RAI car series which was operated by clockwork and offered several interchangeable bodies, e.g. a saloon car, a sports car, a bus, a truck or an ambulance. They were presented in an assortment box of ten different models.

# Alphabetical description
# of the German firms

*Arnold*

In 1906, in Nuremberg, Karl Arnold started producing tin-plate toys with a built-in flint. A special patent protected these cheap novelty toys. In the years before the Second World War the Arnold collection contained small boats, submarines, fire-engines and steam-engine accessories. Apart from a standstill during the First World War, tin-plate toys were produced until the late fifties. After Karl Arnold's death in 1946, the management was taken over by a son-in-law, Christian Ernst. In those days the firm produced particularly such toys as clockwork cars, tractors, etc. In the 1960s Arnold introduced a range of 'Rapido' N gauge model trains.

*Biller*

In 1937 Hans Biller, a former co-worker of Bing-Werke, started a business of his own in Nuremberg. Biller was known for his clockwork railway sets. After the Second World War he also produced cranes and helicopters, but the railway sets were the most important items. At the beginning of the sixties Biller also switched to plastic as a basic material. The firm is still in business.

*Bing*  a  b   c  d  e

In 1863 Ignaz and Adolf Bing started a wholesale business in household goods and toys in Nuremberg under the name 'Gebrüder Bing'. In 1879 they started production on their own, although they did business with a large number of people working part-time. They also changed the name of the firm into 'Nürnberger Metall- und Lackierwaarenfabrik Gebrüder Bing'.

Trademark *a* was introduced in the 1890s. The initial trademark *b* was used on toys during the period 1900–19. The intertwined initials G.B., trademark *c*, also indicated a Bing toy. In 1919 the B.W. trademark was introduced. These trademarks were often embossed on the tin-plate or stamped on a separate metal plate fixed to the toy.

In 1919 Ignaz Bing, one of the founders, died. One of the first actions of his successor was the establishment of 'Concentra', their own sales organization. Stephan Bing, who was in charge now, gave all his energy to extending the firm. Several divisions of Concentra, including stocks and sample-rooms, were established in a great number of European countries. Concentra divisions were also set up outside Europe. During the First World War Bing worked on many orders for the army and increased their staff.

In 1920 Bing had about 10,000 workers, three or four thousand of whom were employed in toy manufacturing.

The Wall Street crash in 1929 brought in another era. In spite of help by the main company, Concentra fell into financial difficulties and although there was an annual sale of about 27 million DM Bing was in serious trouble. The high production levels and the large and confused assortment of products proved disastrous for Bing. Stephan Bing had to leave the firm and a receiver was appointed. In 1932 the production of tin-plate toys was stopped. Karl Bub took over some of the production equipment; thus the Bing trademark was used in 1933 for the last time incorporated with the Bub trademark.

Bing's collection included not only tin-plate toys, like cars, ships, trains, trams, etc., but also optical and electrical material, such as steam-engines, hot-air motors, magic lanterns and stereoscopes.

*Blomer and Schüler*

In 1919 the production of clockwork mechanisms was in progress in a small factory in Nuremberg. About 1930 they started the production of mechanical tin-plate toys. The first item they introduced was an elephant, named 'Jumbo', which is still to be found in the trademark. A small collection of animals was put on the market and produced until the Second World War. After 1947 mainly roundabouts and some helicopters were produced. In 1974 they decided to stop production.

*Bolz*

In 1875 Lorenz Bolz founded his firm in Zirndorf. In 1880 he started the production of zinc tops but gradually Bolz switched over to using tin-plate as basic material. Their exports went mainly to the United States. In 1913 they developed the top with pump mechanism, followed in 1924 by the introduction of the first 4-note chords top. The technique was developed and in 1937 Bolz showed a humming-top with 20-note chords.

After the Second World War, Paul Henkel, a son-in-law of the founder, took over the management along with his wife

Anni. Besides the humming-top production, which was approximately 90 per cent of the total sales, Bolz also manufactured tinplate musical boxes and toys for use in the summer, such as buckets, spades and watering cans. The new safety regulations in their country were partly the reason Bolz switched over to using plastic. Nowadays Bolz is still one of the leading hummingtop manufacturers in the world.

Brandstätter

In 1876 Andreas Brandstätter founded a firm of the same name. He started by producing cashbox mountings and locks. This was gradually followed by the introduction of tin-plate toys, for example, money-boxes and toy telephones. After the Second World War plastic became the main material used in toy manufacturing. At the present time the 'GEOBRA' trademark is managed by Horst and Michael Brandstätter.

Bub

In 1851, in Nuremberg, Karl Bub started producing tin-plate toys with or without clockwork. About 1905 he started producing clockwork trains and electric specimens were introduced before the First World War.

In 1933 Bub took over a big part of Bing-Werke. In the catalogue of the same year Bub put his own initials next to those of Bing. Clockwork cars were also favourite items. During the Second World War the factory was hit several times, but they started to rebuild and Bub introduced an electric train in gauge S; this gauge S = 22 mm. It was a failure and even switching the gauge did not prove to be successful. Bub stopped production in 1966 and in 1967 an American, Frank Tarr, took over the name of the firm.

*Bühler*

In 1860 the firm Bühler was formed by the Bühler Brothers at Triberg in the Black Forest. The factory produced milled toy clockworks. In 1924 they decided to set up a division in Nuremberg, because they were too far away from their clients such as Bing, Hess, Tipp and Schuco.

In 1927 Bühler used the coil-spring clockwork for the first time, followed in 1929 by a friction mechanism. Over the years many variations have been made. According to the wishes of the manufacturers the standard clockwork mechanisms ranged in size from 0·2 mm to 0·35 mm. Nowadays clockworks are still made and Bühler's trademark (a spruce-fir) is to be seen on many keys and clockworks.

*Carette*

In 1886 the Frenchman George Carette started production in Nuremberg under the name 'George Carette et Cie.'. As his partner Hopf had connections with Bing, Carette became an early supplier of Bing, but later on he went his own way. At the International Exhibition of 1893 he was the first manufacturer who offered an electric tram. Paul Josephtal, his new partner, had connections with an English colleague, Wenman Bassett-Lowke. A sort of co-operative began and Carette manufactured all the railway-carriages and even some locomotive models for Bassett-Lowke. By about 1910 Carette was also producing clockwork cars and boats. The folding windscreen and hand brake were particular details on some model cars.

After the outbreak of the First World War, Carette had to flee to his native country, because he was still a French citizen. In spite of all the efforts made by Josephtal, the factory had to close in 1917. The founder died in the twenties in France.

*Distler*

In 1900 Johann Distler decided to start production in Nuremberg. In 1923 the founder died and the direction the firm was to take was guided by Braun and Meyer. The pre-1914 tin-plate toys offered were penny-toy road vehicles. In 1935/36 the members of the board had to flee to England for political reasons.

'Turn-over' car no. 310
(Distler)

Ernst Völk took over the Distler production and two years later he also took over Trix. In spite of some good years after the Second World War production stopped in 1962. At that time the collection consisted of cars, planes, railway stations and novelty toys.

46

## Doll

In 1898 tinsmith Peter Doll started with his partner J. Sondheim. In the early years they manufactured all sorts of stationary steam-engines and accessories. About 1927 the expert Reichel joined the Doll team from Bing. Not only steam engines, but also novelty toys and trains were produced. In 1938 the Doll production was taken over by the bigger Nuremberg firm of Fleischmann. At that time Doll was managed by Max Bein and J. Sondheim. Fleischmann still continued to make trains under the Doll trademark.

## Eberl

Hans Eberl was the founder of this Nuremberg firm. In 1902 the board of directors was formed by Ludwig and Emil Schwarzbauer. The collection consisted of several attractive cars and novelty toys. The Eberl firm was officially liquidated in 1929.

## Einfalt

In 1922 the brothers Georg and Johann Einfalt founded the Einfalt firm in Nuremberg. Until 1935 some of their clockwork novelty toys were marked by the initials G.E.N.; then they changed it to 'Technofix' and it became their trademark. In

Butterfly (Einfalt), c. 1930

*Man on floats (Einfalt), c. 1930*

those days the export to Switzerland and Sweden was very important. The collection included tin-plate animals, cars (some without a clockwork), spiral railways, aeroplanes and some steam-rollers with a clockwork mechanism. After the Second World War they continued the old collection. Then gradually plastic became their basic material. At the present time their sons Alfred and Johann control the firm.

*Falk*

In 1897 Joseph Falk, a former employee of Carette, decided to work for himself. The lion's share of the Falk collection was formed by steam-engines including accessories and magic lanterns. By taking over a share of the bankrupt firm of Jean Schönner, Falk expanded his own collection of ships, submarines and trains. In 1935 the firm was taken over by Ernst Plank; otherwise the whole business would have been forfeited.

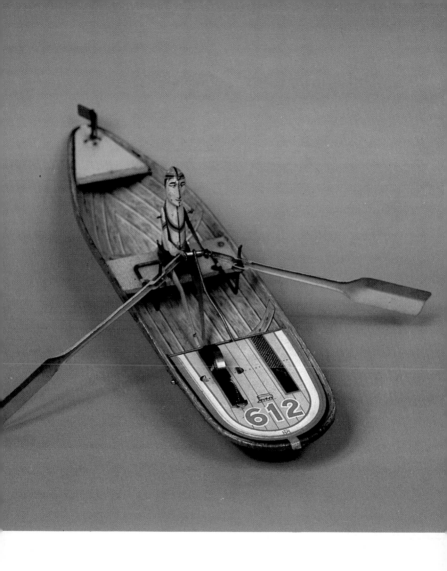

Wind-up rowing boat with oarsman no. 612 (Payà), 1946.

*Top*  Ocean steamer no. 750/3 (Arnold) and boat with propeller no. 1600 (Arnold), both with wind-up mechanism, and steamer no. 902 (Fleischmann).

*Bottom*  Warship (probably Carette).

*Top* Wind-up paddleboat (Uebelacker), c. 1900.

*Bottom* Wind-up motorboat (JEP).

Water-plane (Payà), 1947.

Monoplane M – 750 (I.N.G.A.P.), 1933, and monoplane no. 613 (I.N.G.A.P.)

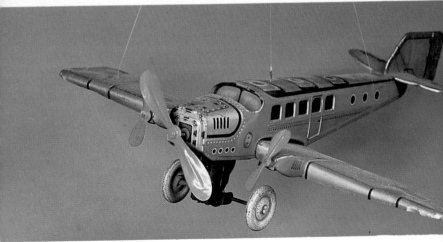

*Top*   Wind-up zeppelin (probably of French manufacture).

*Bottom*   Triple-engined monoplane (probably of German manufacture).

Stuntflyer no. 600 (Günthermann), c. 1938. The plane moves around in a circle on the ground after the spring has been wound up.

Amusement park 'dipper' (Blomer and Schüler), 1950.

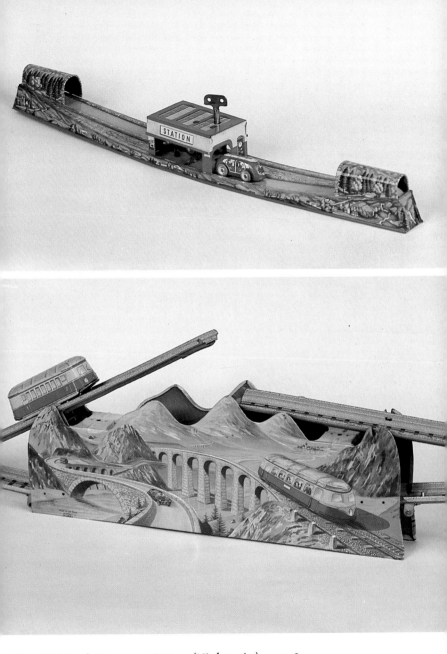

*Top*   Tick-Tack Express no. PN 500 (Niedermeier), c. 1948.

*Bottom*   Mountain Express no. 252 (Einfalt), 1948.

*Above*  Station no. 74/2 (Schönner), 1900, and wind-up locomotive no. 980 with tender, carriage no. 1882 and goods wagon no. 1883 in gauge O (Märklin), 1924.

*Top right*  Wind-up train with two carriages marked with the destination Paris – Moscow and a goods wagon (Faivre) 1880 – 1890.

*Bottom right*  Electric locomotive no. CER. 65/13021 in gauge 1 (Märklin), 1919. Tap-Tap no. 560 (Lehmann), 1912, is in the foreground.

Restaurant-car no. 1932 in gauge 1 (Märklin), c. 1925, signal clock no. 2244 and signals (Märklin), 1929.

Station no. 2010 (Märklin), 1919, and wind-up tram no. 10244 in gauge O (Bing), 1912.

Fire engine S.P. without mechanism (of French manufacture), 1935. This model was also produced with a wire-spring mechanism, front bumper, running boards and mudguards.

Tip-up truck no. 122 (Tipp), 1936, and in front a wind-up steam-roller (Oro-Werke), c. 1920.

Various cars. Among them, Hessmobiel no. 1022 (Hess) c. 1914; lorry no. 518 (Gundka), c. 1925; taxi no. 975 (Rossignol), 1930; double-decker bus no. 119 (Rico), 1934; open car with leather folding hood and driver (Carette), c. 1910; landaulette with wire-spring mechanism (of German manufacture), c. 1910; double-decker bus no. 131 (Wells), 1946; racing car made of hammered tin-plated iron no. 632 D7 (Distler), 1933; and a Shell filling station (Pratts and Letchworth).

Fire-engine no. J.D. 3701 (Distler), c. 1933.

'Tut-Tut' no. 490 (Lehmann), 1906.

A toy similar to that opposite, but the man with the horn is now the passenger in the side-car of a motor cycle no. 1 – 804 (Payà), 1933.

Hand painted collapsible castle. In front is a racing car no. 820 (Tipp), 1936.

Penny toy cars and plane (among them toys made by Einfalt, G.L.B. Italy, Fischer).

Cast iron ladder-truck (probably Hubley), c. 1900.

Motor cycle with rubber tyres, c. 1910.

*Above*  'Echo' motorcyclist no. 725 (Lehmann), 1918.
*Top right*  Four Lehmann toys. From left to right: Zulu no. 721, 1910; obstinate donkey no. 524, 1921; Onkel no. 345, 1917; and Zirka no. 752, 1913.
*Bottom right*  Five motorcyclists: motorcycle with side-car no. 587 (Tipp); motor-

cycle no T. 586 (Tipp); motorcycle TCO – 59 (Tipp); motorcycle, with flint mechanism in the headlight, no. A 643 (Arnold) and motorcycle no. GE 255 (Einfalt), 1950.

Mr. and Mrs. Lehmann (Lehmann), c. 1890. Driven by friction.

Cyclist (probably of French manufacture) c. 1890. This model had to be pushed forward by inserting a little stick into the holder behind the saddle.

Copy of the Lehmann toy opposite, no. 1-952 (Payà), 1931.

Peter the Clown no. 503 (Lehmann), 1914.

Motorised clown (Märklin), 1909.

Clown at easel (of German manufacture), c. 1895. By turning the handle, interchangeable discs connected to the clown's hands start to move so that he sketches the portrait of an historical figure on the paper. In this case it is Joséphine de Beauharnais, but there were also discs for Napoleon and Louis XIV.

Little boy with cap (Joustra).

Mirako Peter the motorcyclist no. 1013 (Schuco), 1955.

Tournament no. 138 (Einfalt), c. 1935.

Biting Bulldog no. 149 (Einfalt), c. 1930.

*Left* Pinocchio on tricycle no. 770 (I.N.G.A.P.), 1936.
*Below* A number of circus figures. Among them: juggling monkey (Kohler), 1948, (far left), and next to it a clown walking on his hands (Kohler), 1948; in the centre a juggling seal (of French manufacture) and, far right, another clown walking on his hands no. 152 (Wells), 1949.

Circus elephant (Nurnberger Blechspielwarenfabrik), 1950.

Group of circus elephants (Nurnberger Blechspielwarenfabrik), 1950.

Turkey (Blomer & Schüler), 1948.

Peacock with real tail feathers (of French manufacture), c. 1900. In front are
two velour peck-peck birds no. 905 (Schuco), 1930.

A collection of tops. The one on the left is a humming top (Nüsslein), 1938.

Accessories driven by steam-engine (Bing), 1902. From left to right: painter no. 8743/1, woman gardening no. 8743/3 and woodcutter no. 8743/6.

The big cannon is probably a cottage industry product; the wooden cannon balls were the ammunition. To show the difference in size the cannon from the opposite page has been photographed next to it. In front of the cannonballs is a little pop-gun.

'Ideal' pea cannon in camouflage colours no. 23/4 (Schrödel), 1934.

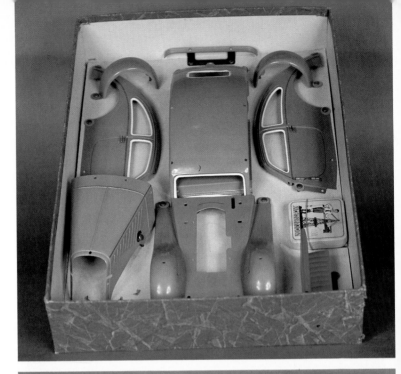

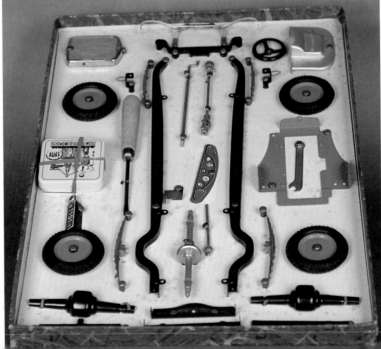

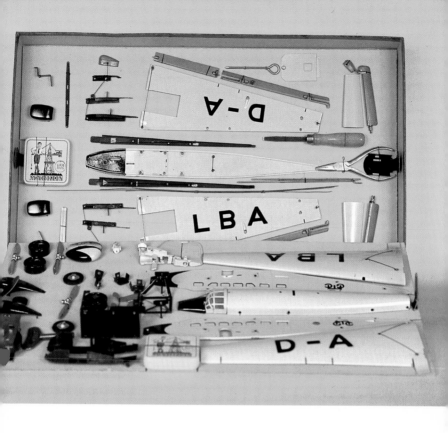

*Above* Aeroplane construction kit of triple-engined Lunkersmodel no. 1152 (Märklin), 1937.
*Left* Car bodywork construction kit no. 1103 ST (Märklin), 1933, and chassis construction kit no. 1101 c (Märklin), 1933.

*Above*  Autogyro no. G. ACUI (T.K.)

*Top right*  One of the oldest trains ever made. Unfortunately the chimney is missing. Made in Germany or France, c. 1880, the voile curtains at the windows of the compartment enhance the charm of this little train.

*Bottom right*  The train's simple spiral spring mechanism. By turning the back wheel the rope is wound around the back axle tightening the spring. The train moves when placed on the ground.

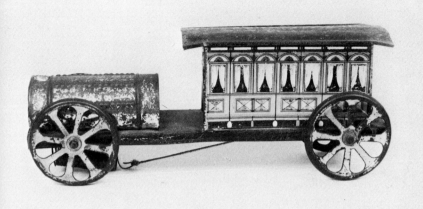

Citroen B2 taxi with driver (Jouets d'André Citroën), 1924.

*Top*   Open tourer car, c. 1910. The lady driver was an unusual sight at that time and the figure possibly depicts a suffragette.
*Bottom*   A close-up of the lady driver. The model was hand painted with a brush.

*Top* Hand painted ambulance, fly wheel driven (C. Rossignol). c. 1900.
*Bottom* Express postman (Saalheimer & Strauss), c. 1930. It could be wound up by turning a key in the hole below the middle of the back wheel.

Lorry 'EHE & Co.' no. 570 (Lehmann), 1912.

*Top* Limousine with rubber tyres and tip-up windscreen (Carette), 1910. There were two brake handles, one on each side on the running boards.
*Bottom* Station no. 13183 (Bing), 1912. In front is wind-up tram no. 206 with spiral spring mechanism.

Traveller with suitcases no. 699 (Distler), 1933.

*Above*   The mysterious ball (Martin), 1906.
*Left*   Gustav the miller no. 230 (Lehmann), 1920.

Mickey Mouse with barrel-organ (Distler), c. 1928.

Felix the cat no. 765 (I.N.G.A.P.), 1936.

Close-up of 'OH – MY' negro's face no. 690 (Lehmann) 1903.

Tap dancer 'OH – MY' no. 690 (Lehmann), 1903, with its original packaging.

Drunken sailor no. 535 (Lehmann), 1910. He can also walk when put upside down on his cap.

*Top*   Submarine (Clément), c. 1895.
*Bottom*   Gun-boat, pleasure yacht and ocean steamer under Dutch flag (Arnold).
All four have a wind-up mechanism.

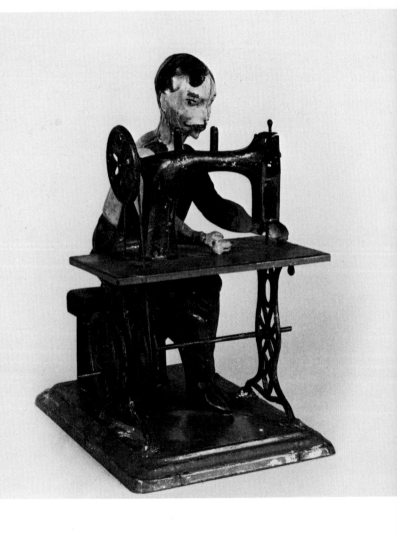

Accessory for machine driven by steam; tailor.

Fireman with ladder (Martin), 1904.

Back of wind-up pulley wagon no. 2431 (Märklin), 1904. The rail was used to control the toy and could be moved by the figures sitting in the back.

Front of the same pulley wagon. The toy figures wear stuff uniforms.

Side view of the wind-up pulley wagon no. 2431 (Märklin), 1904.

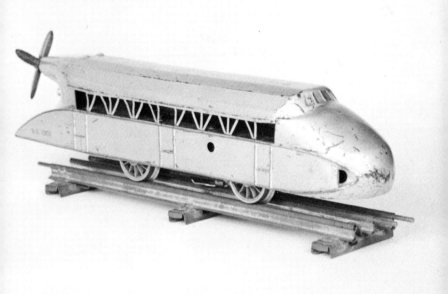

*Top*  Wind-up model of an American train in gauge O (Issmayer), c. 1895.
*Bottom*  Electric rail zeppelin no. SZ 12970 in gauge O (Märklin), 1931.

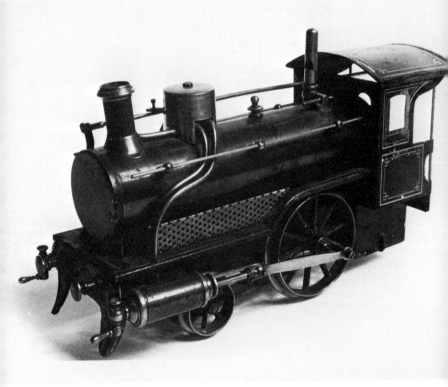

*Top*  Wind-up locomotive no. B 1021 with tender in gauge O (Märklin), 1909;
*Bottom*  Steam locomotive no. 118 SR in gauge 2 (Schönner), 1905.

Station no. 647/32 (Carette), c. 1900.

*Top* 'NA – NU' no. 752 (Lehmann), c. 1930.
*Bottom* Chinese carriers (Lehmann), c. 1902.

*Top* 'ALSO' delivery vans no. 700 (Lehmann), 1925.
*Bottom* The original cardboard packing for these vans.

Clown in action (Fischer), c. 1925.

Gentleman with walking stick (C.K.).

*Top right*   Chestnut seller with stuff apron (Martin), c. 1900.
*Top left*   Couple walzing, with stuff clothes (Martin), 1888.
*Bottom*   Billiard player pocketing a glass ball into a hole on the table (Kienberger), 1913.

Hunter with rifle at the ready. When the lever is pulled he puts his rifle on the ground.

*Top* Pea cannon (Hess), c. 1930.
*Below* Steam-driven warship with double propellers (Bing), c. 1902. This ship is about 80 cm (32 in) long and 43 cm (17 in) high.

Detail of the poop deck with artillery of the ship on the page opposite.

*Above* Wind-up ball, Bismarck no. 764 (Lehmann), 1930. To the left is the mechanism; the weight fastened eccentrically makes the ball roll to all sides.
*Below* Incomplete humming top (Fuchs), c. 1930.

*Fischer*

In 1903 Georg Fischer started the production of tin-plate toys in Nuremberg. His assorted collection contained small and simple mechanical toys (with or without a clockwork mechanism). 80 per cent of the collection was exported before the First World War. The last time Fischer was listed in the directory was 1958.

*Little girl with dog no. 55 (Georg Fischer), c. 1930*

*Fischer*

H. Fischer & Co. was known as a Nuremberg toy manufacturer of trains, but his collection also included accessories and cars. In

*Tractor no. 92W (Georg Fischer), c. 1930*

all probability Fischer manufactured the first toy cars with battery-operated headlights. Fischer commenced production about 1908 and went bankrupt in 1931/32, because of an incorrect calculation on a small clockwork train set.

*Fleischmann*

In 1887 Jean Fleischmann started in Nuremberg with the production of floating, magnetic tin-plate toys such as geese, ducks, fish and small boats. A little piece of iron was soldered into the mouth of the creature or in the front of the boat and, by means of a magnet, it was possible to pull the toys through the water. Later on clockwork mechanisms were used.

In 1917 the founder died and his wife Käthe and his brother continued the business. From 1920 all Fleischmann toys were fitted with a trademark. In 1928 the firm Georg Staudt was taken over by Fleischmann; Staudt had had to stop production because he had no successor. Fleischmann took over roundabouts with built-in musical boxes and mechanical figures like dancing clowns, etc.

In 1938 Fleischmann decided to increase their collection by taking over a lot of Doll models.

In 1940 the sons Johann and Emil Fleischmann took over and their only interest became the production of trains. They are still manufacturing trains. In 1948 they introduced their electric gauge 0. In 1952 Fleischmann started the production of ships and in 1968 also steam-engines.

*Förtner und Haffner*

This firm was founded by Andreas Förtner and Joh. Haffner in Nuremberg. They started in the beginning of the twenties and their collection consisted of flat tin soldiers, rolling bells, children's scales, etc. In 1927 the firm was taken over by Stephan Bing and others; the firm's name was changed to 'Vereinigte Spielwarenfabrik'. With the introduction of the Trix construction kits, the name was changed to 'Trix'. (For more information see under Trix).

*Fuchs* MFZ

In 1919 Martin Fuchs started in Zirndorf, a little village near Nuremberg. Until 1925 he manufactured goods such as celluloid baby rattles.

The next stage in development was the manufacture of zinc tops which were hand-made and painted. Fuchs also extended his collection by taking over some Bing articles, such as some roundabouts and a ferris-wheel. The last hand-made humming-tops disappeared about 1935 and tin-plate became the basic material. In 1947 his son Friedrich joined the firm. In 1950 his father retired, and died in 1953. Toys exported from Fuchs were always sold by way of the wholesale trade. From the beginning all the Fuchs models were labelled. At the present time humming-tops still represent the most important part of the collection. Peter and Eberhard Fuchs are the present directors.

*Gundka*

The Gundka-Werke operated in Brandenburg. This firm, owned by Greppert & Kelch, went bankrupt in the thirties. It seems that a certain Mr. Hille took over the firm and production continued until about 1944.

*Günthermann*

The founder, S. Günthermann, started in 1877 by manufacturing tin-plate toys in Nuremberg. He died in 1890 leaving his wife and two sons Christian and Leonhard behind. It did not mean the end of the firm, however; the business was continued by Arnold Weigel, who meanwhile had married the widow of Günthermann. He made it his task to enlarge the collection with such toys as cars, racing cars, tram-cars, aeroplanes, etc. Up to 1914 even, 65 per cent of their collection was exported to the United States. Weigel died in 1919 and Leonhard Günthermann took charge. In the Second World War the factory was destroyed several times. In 1951 it was rebuilt for the last time and fourteen years later Günthermann jr. decided to retire on account of his old age, and the factory was closed.

*Hausser*

This toy firm, particularly known as Elastolin (their known trademark), was founded in 1904 by the brothers Otto and Max Hausser in Ludwigsburg, not far from Stuttgart. Their trademark 'Elastolin' was introduced in 1926. In the years between 1935 and 1940 Hausser manufactured some interesting tin-plate toys besides their main product, elastolin figures. Elastolin was a composite material comprising plaster, sawdust and glue over a wire base. Military toys were very popular in those days in Germany and Hausser manufactured some superb army trucks, guns, etc. In a toy catalogue there was a magnificent half-track troop carrier, no. 731. The cloth roof could be folded back and there was room for a driver and ten elastolin soldiers. The model had a spring motor and electric lights. In 1936 the firm was transferred to Neustadt. During 1930–40 their elastolin figures were also sold by Märklin as an accessory to their train sets in gauges o and 1. Their collection stayed that way until 1955 when Hausser switched over to using plastic.

*Heller & Schiller*

Before the Second World War Heller & Schiller was domiciled at Obersleutensdorf in Sudetenland. Nowadays this village is in Czechoslavakia and called Litvinov. Their collection, under the trademark 'HUSCH', consisted of such things as buckets and spades, cars, trucks, tram-cars, little trains and aeroplanes. In 1942 Heller & Schiller were forced to turn their production towards making war materials. After 1945 nothing more was heard about this firm.

*Hess*

Mattheus Hess belonged undoubtedly to one of the oldest toy manufacturers of Nuremberg and Germany. The firm was founded in 1826 and Hess was one of the first manufacturers to produce trains without a clockwork mechanism. A few years later they also manufactured clockwork trains. In 1866 Johann took over the running of the company after the death of his father and increased sale. The firm Hess derived their reputation from their 'Hessmobiel' (clockwork cars). In 1934 Johann Hess died and the factory had to close.

*Höfler*

In 1938 Johann Höfler started manufacturing toys in Fürth. He produced tin-plate toys run by clockwork, particularly mechanical animals and tracks. Production of these lasted until 1954, when Ernst Bettag changed the whole output. From then on the firm was called 'Big' and only manufactured plastic toys.

*Issmayer*

In 1861 Johann Andr. Issmayer started on his own, after working for a while with his father. At the beginning he manufactured floating, magnetic tin-plate toys and some children's cooking-ranges. Gradually he increased the production of trains, many of which went to the United States. In 1922 the founder died and J. Weissgerber, a son-in-law, took over the business. He died in 1926 and his son August became director of Issmayer. Unfortunately, he could not prevent its closure in 1933/34. The exact date is unknown.

*Keim*

In 1937/38 the Nuremberg firm Keim & Co. took over the Jewish firm 'Kraus & Co.'. After the Second World War Keim manufactured simple clockwork trains in gauge 0. They continued their collection until 1960 when they ceased production.

*Kellermann*

In 1910 Georg Kellermann started business in Nuremberg and three years later took a partner. Kellermann himself specialized in the production of the so-called penny toys. Later on they put simple mechanical toys on the market, with or without a clockwork mechanism. In 1924 his son, Willy, joined his father and took over in 1931 after his father's death.

Nearly the whole collection was exported in those days. This changed, however, in about 1935. During the Second World War they produced war materials. After the war they exported their small collection. In 1960 Willy's son, Helmuth, became sales promotor, and nowadays Kellermann still manufacture tin-plate toys, driven by friction.

*Kienberger*

At the end of 1910 Hubert Kienberger founded a firm in Nuremberg for the production of penny toys and simple mechanical tin-plate toys. The collection contained such items as ladder-trucks or covered wagons pulled by horses, lambs and donkeys on wheels. A few months later, Georg Levy became a partner and the name of the firm changed to 'Kienberger & Co.'. A billiard player introduced by Kienberger became a real hit, with 90 per cent of sales to the export market. In 1916 both partners separated and Levy started on his own. In the twenties the Kienberger collection consisted of trains, cars and motor-cyclists. The chosen trademark 'HUKI' was formed by the first two letters of the founder's name. He died in 1938 and his daughter Irmgard took over the management. The factory was bombed out in 1943, but production restarted in 1949. At the present time a grandson of Kienberger is director.

*Kindler & Briel*

In 1865 the firm Kindler & Briel was founded by Wilhelm Kindler at Böblingen. At that time the toy collection contained wooden and tin-plate toys. Much of this was exported long before the First World War, the most important buyers being Switzerland, England and the United States.

After the death of Wilhelm Kindler his sons, Willy and Paul, took over the business. Production increased and they decided to specialize in tin-plate railway accessories. In the Second World War toy production stagnated and in the last days of the war the plants were destroyed. After 1945 Kindler & Briel worked hard to rebuild their company and plastic became the basic material for their toy manufacture. There was a form of co-operation between Distler and Kindler & Briel, whereby they combined to use certain garage presses which were adjusted to the Distler cars.

*Köhler*

In 1932 Georg Köhler started the production, on a small scale, of mechanical tin-plate animals and until the Second World War the collection remained unaltered. During the war production was stopped by lack of material, but after 1948 Köhler enlarged his collection and bigger sales resulted. Köhler is still active in this field.

*Kraus*

In 1910 Josef Kraus started producing clockwork trains which were followed by electric copies a few years later. Until 1930 particularly, exports were important. The trademark used, 'FANDOR', was a combination of the first three letters of Josef Kraus' mother and aunt, namely Fanny and Dora. Later the home-market became more important. In 1933 Josef Kraus left Germany (under pressure from the Nazi regime) and emigrated to the United States. Keim & Co. took over production in 1937/38, but it was only a postponement of closure, because in 1939 production stopped completely.

*Krauss*

In 1895 Wilhelm Krauss founded a small factory for the production of tin-plate toys in Nuremberg. The collection consisted of roundabouts with aeroplanes (spindle movement), tractors, etc. The last time the firm was listed in the directory was in 1938. In that year Krauss sold his toy firm to Keim & Co.

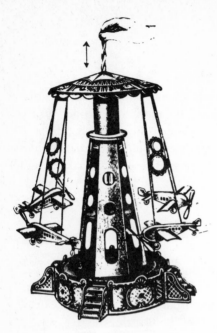

*Merry-go-round no. 341/1 (W. Krauss), 1937*

*Lehmann*

a

b

Ernst Paul Lehmann, the founder, started producing tin-plate toys with fly-wheel mechanisms in Brandenburg in 1881. He developed the coil-spring mechanism. His cousin Johann Richter joined the firm in 1911; until then Lehmann toys were labelled with trademark *a*. Then the initials EPL were combined (trademark *b*). In 1913 Lehmann produced another novelty, the first one-rail railway, which was followed by another in 1921, namely an amphibious vehicle called 'UHU'.

In 1934 the founder died and was succeeded by Johann Richter. In those days Lehmann ran short of material and were forced to manufacture smaller toys, the so-called Gnome series.

Lehmann became one of the leading toy manufacturers in the world. During the Second World War production continued for a long time, the toys being sold to neutral countries. After the war they started again, but under Russian supervision. In 1947 Johann Richter gave up his possessions and fled with his family to the Western Zone. In 1951 he started in Nuremberg again with his sons. They had to rebuild a new collection because they had left everything behind. Tom the climbing monkey, the Gnome tops, the Na-Nu and the cable-railway were the only old items. These Lehmann articles were different in size, and the lacquer finish used was different from the articles produced before the two world wars.

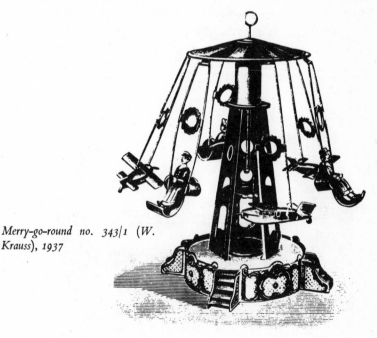

*Merry-go-round no. 343/1 (W. Krauss), 1937*

In 1956 Johann Richter died and his sons Eberhard and Wolfgang took over the management. Meanwhile in Brandenburg the 'Volkseigener Betrieb Mechanische Spielwaren' also continued the production of tin-plate toys. The present Lehmann collection still consists of tin-plate novelty toys with a clockwork or friction mechanism and, since 1968, the plastic LGB railway.

*Levy*

Up to 1916 Georg Levy was joint proprietor of Hubert Kienberger's toy factory. In 1920/21 he started his own production in Nuremberg and sold his goods to exporters and wholesale dealers. In 1934 Levy had to sell up for political reasons. He fled with his family to England and settled down in London. The firm continued to exist under the name 'Nürnberger Blechspielwarenfabrikation' and was managed by Karl Ochs. Despite his efforts he could not prevent the closure of the factory in 1971.

*Billiards players no. 50 (Levy), c. 1925*

*Lineol*

This Brandenburg firm, managed by Oskar Wiederholz, started production in 1934. The arrival of Russian troops in 1945 put an end to the firm. The Lineol collection consisted mainly of military vehicles with a clockwork mechanism, completed by elastolin soldiers.

*Mangold*     **GAMA**

Georg Adam Mangold started production of mechanical tin-plate animals on 2 January 1882 in Fuerth. In 1920 his son Hans took over and expanded the firm. Their 'GAMA' trademark was introduced about 1924. Until the Second World War about

*Advertisement for Mangold in Fürth*

70 per cent of their collection was exported to other countries.

During the war toy manufacture was stopped in order to make war materials.

At the end of 1945 they started again on a small scale and with the currency reform soon turned the corner. In 1948 they were already exporting. In those days, shortly after the war, some Schuco items were made under licence by Mangold such as the turn-over car no. 100. The present-day collection includes cranes, tractors, model cars and racetracks. In 1971 the Trix firm was added to the Gama concern.

*Markes*

In 1904 Carl Markes founded Markes & Co. in Lüdenscheid. They began by producing bicycle accessories, and then in 1932 introduced tin-plate toys under the 'DUX' trademark. These were mainly model car and aeroplane construction kits, some of which were clockwork driven. After the Second World War a construction kit like Meccano completed the collection, but plastic took the place of the old basic material.

*Märklin*

Theodore F. Märklin was born in 1817. In 1859 he started manufacturing with his wife in Göppingen a number of toys such as children's cooking-ranges. After the death of her husband in 1866 Karoline continued the firm. A few years later she also died and her sons Karl, Wilhelm and Eugen had to continue penniless. In 1880 the name changed to 'Gebrüder Märklin'. Among the toys they manufactured were doll's carriages, ships, merry-go-rounds, zeppelins and humming-tops. Their first

*Railway snowplough no.
1890 (Märklin), 1929*

trains consisted of locomotives with carriages, but without rails.
They had to be pulled along on a string. This meant the start of
the production of model toy trains.

In 1892 the name became 'Gebrüder Märklin & Cie.', with
the addition of Emil Fiz and later Richard Safft to the board of
directors. Before the First World War, Märklin manufactured
the Meccano system under licence.

In 1923 Fritz Märklin, a son of Eugen Märklin joined the
firm after he had worked for several years in the United States.
In 1935 Eugen retired and Fritz took up the expansion of the
Märklin concern until his death in 1961. In 1934 Märklin
launched car construction kits in several versions, followed by an
aeroplane kit in 1937. After 1946 the production of car construction kits continued until 1953. Märklin had to make war
materials in both World Wars. At the beginning of the fifties
an end came to the mass-production of tin-plate trains. Since
then only plastic trains have been manufactured.

*Meier*

In 1879 Johann Philipp Meier founded his toy firm in Nuremberg. In 1894 he registered his trademark 'dog with cart'. By

the end of the century Johann Meier had succeeded in developing his factory, where so-called penny toys were manufactured, into one of the leading Nuremberg firms. Exports were handled via the wholesale trade. Several 'Meier penny toys' in the well-known penny toy collection of Ernst King can be seen in the Victoria and Albert Museum in London. Johann Meier died in 1911 and Jean Weinberger took over the management of the firm.

*Moschkowitz*

In spring 1919 Max Moschkowitz founded a toy firm in Nuremberg. He started with a small collection of mechanical tin-plate toys and in 1929 he established a division in England. In 1921 he introduced his trademark for the first time. During the Second World War production in his German factory ceased. After 1948 he re-started and continued until 1971 when he decided to close down his German factory.

### Neuhierl

In 1920 Joseph Neuhierl founded his firm in Fürth. Tin-plate toys, especially car models, were produced until 1956. The letters JNF indicated their trademark. Plastic toys came into fashion and in 1963 Neuhierl introduced the 'Carrera race-track'.

### Niedermeier

In 1934 Philipp Niedermeier took over the toy firm Saalheimer & Strauss in Nuremberg. Tin-plate 'trumpets' were the main items produced in those days before the Second World War. In 1946 Niedermeier introduced their trademark with Nuremberg tower. Clockwork toys on tracks were manufactured mainly until 1960 when the firm moved to Parsberg. The directors then decided to stop production of mechanical tin-plate toys because of the competition from Japan and Hong Kong.

*Nürnberger Blechspielwarenfabrik*
See under *Levy*.

*Nüsslein*

On 4 November 1889, Michael Müsslein founded the firm which bore his name. He had gained some experience before by working in a metal-printing factory for a number of years. In 1922 he took his son Ludwig into partnership. His collection consisted of humming-tops, music-boxes, rolling bells and magic lanterns. These articles were always sold by wholesale dealers in Nuremberg and Fürth. In 1964 they decided to close down the factory in Zirndorf.

*Oro-Werke*

The partners Reil, Blechschmidt and Müller had a firm in Brandenburg, and manufactured tin-plate toys until 1922.

*Plank*

In 1866 Ernst Plank founded his firm in Nuremberg. At the beginning only steam-engines and magic lanterns were manufactured. About 1890 the first steam-trains were added to the collection, later followed by clockwork specimens. In 1882

Plank probably invented the first electric toy train. He produced another novelty, a sort of amphibious vehicle, in 1914. An amphibious boat on four wheels, this clockwork vehicle operated as well on the floor as it sailed in the water. Only Lehmann made a big hit with his version a few years later.

Plank got into financial straits in the thirties and the firm was taken over by the Schaller Brothers. They specialized in manufacturing film-projectors.

*Rissmann*

In 1907 William Rissmann reported the take-over of Martin Ettinger's toy factory in Nuremberg. He was well known for his clockwork train sets.

*Rohrseitz*

In 1881 Karl Rohrseitz founded his firm in Zirndorf. At first Rohrseitz manufactured rattles in zinc or brass, which were nickel-plated. Shortly after the turn of the century his son Fritz joined the company and handled the export of practically the whole collection of rattles. During the First World War export was at a standstill and after 1918 the market changed and so Rohrseitz started manufacturing tin-plate musical boxes. They became popular items, and were soon being exported to England and America. Money-boxes and 'seaside' toys such as watering-cans, buckets and moulds were added to the collection. In 1925 Rohrseitz introduced his trademark. In 1930, the humming-top, which became the most important Rohrseitz item, was introduced. These tops were available in various sizes. Pictures were lithographed on the top. After the Second World War only the

*Diver no. 470 (Plank), 1914*

humming-tops and money-boxes continued to be manufactured. Plastic replaced tin-plate for reasons of safety and to the present day Rohrseitz still manufactures humming-tops.

*Schönner*

In 1875 Jean Schönner started manufacturing mechanical and optical toys in Nuremberg. At first he offered several magic lanterns and later followed these up with steam-engines. The first-known Schönner train was to be seen in a catalogue of 1887; it was a steam-train for the American market and included a cow-catcher, bell and headlight. The train also had a tender and was available in two gauges, 65 and 115 mm. Schönner also manufactured trains driven by clockwork. His railway accessories consisted of stations, signals, bridges, etc. A few years later, Schönner started producing steam ships, particularly armed ships. In 1904 a second factory was built in Muggendorf and the board of directors included Adolf Dihlmann. In 1910 Schönner closed, and a part of the collection was taken over by Falk.

*Schreyer & Co.*     *Schuco*

In 1912 the firm Schuco was founded by Heinrich Müller and his partner Schreyer. The name of the Nuremberg firm derived from the first letters of Schreyer & Co.

In spite of the departure of Schreyer a few years later, the name of the firm remained unaltered. In the beginning only toy cars were manufactured. About 1920 the collection was expanded with a new kind of toy, namely tin-plate toys which were entirely or partly covered with plush. Animals especially,

*Section through the 'peck-peck' bird (Schuco), 1935*

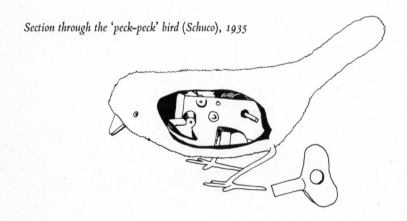

*Advertisement for Schreyer & Co., 1913*

such as bears, monkeys and birds, were produced. In 1929 the world-famous peck-peck bird was shown to the public.

The Bühler clockworks which had been used were changed to Schuco versions. About 1934 it was Schuco who produced the first toy car made in one piece. Another unusual point about the car was that it could not fall from the table because of a specially constructed fifth wheel.

During the Second World War some toys were still manufactured. In the fifties they decided to stop production of the well-known Schuco toy cars.

In 1958 the founder, Heinrich Müller, died and the firm was taken over by his son, Werner, and Alexander Girz. At the present time Schuco is still in the toy business.

*Schrödel*

In 1846 Johann Schrödel started a book-binding firm and carton factory in Nuremberg. After a couple of years they started manufacturing games. Around the turn of the century Schrödel went into the manufacture of toys, specializing in the field of shooting-games. Their trademark 'IDEAL' was printed on their tin-plate toy guns, rifles and pistols. After the Second World War plastic was used more and more as the basic material. At the present time Schrödel is under the management of G. Meidenbauer.

*Schuhmann*

The firm of Adolf Schuhmann produced simple tin-plate toys such as trains. He started about 1925 and perhaps even before

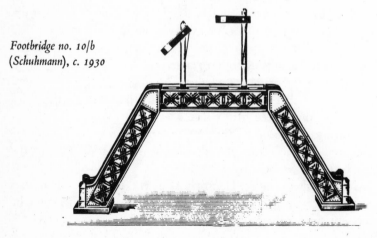

*Footbridge no. 10/b*
*(Schuhmann), c. 1930*

then. His collection contained simple railways (with or without a clockwork), railway accessories, construction kits and cars. This Jewish firm appears to have closed down at the end of the thirties, for Schuhmann is not listed in the directory of 1940.

*Seidel*

In 1881 Michael Seidel founded a toy firm in Nuremberg. A capricorn was introduced as a trademark about the turn of the century. The toy collection before the First World War consisted of tin-plate rattles. Later on, children's tea-sets, money-boxes and toy telephones were added to the Seidel collection. In 1908 Georg Seidel, a son of the founder, took over the management and enlarged the collection to include such toys as clock-work boats, tractors with trailers and some tanks. The Seidel firm had to make war materials in both World Wars. In 1939, Gerhard Hamann, a brother-in-law, joined the board of directors. In 1949 Seidel started producing small steam boats, driven by candle in the beginning as there was a shortage of mechanisms. Later on they were replaced by clockwork mechanisms. In the second half of the fifties even Seidel switched over to the use of plastic as the basic material.

*Staudt*

Between 1840 and 1850 Georg Leonhard Staudt founded a firm, in which tin-plate toys were manufactured. In 1887, his sixteen-year-old son, Heinrich, became an apprentice. About the turn of the century the Staudt toy collection consisted of mechanical tin-plate ships, roundabouts, musical clowns, bears and some aeroplanes; in those days no trains or cars were produced. In 1928 Fleischmann took over the firm because there was no successor.

*Stock & Co*

In 1905 the firm Stock & Co. was founded in Solingen by Walter Stock. This firm became known for its copies of Lehmann models. Stock not only manufactured tin-plate toys, but also Christmas articles, such as tin-plate cribs. Small clockwork cars were also added to the collection.

Production had to stop in the thirties and later on the Stock toy firm was taken over by Paul Hartkopf, who managed a toy firm under his own name.

*Tipp*

The firm Tipp & Co. in Nuremberg was founded in 1912. The name of the firm derived from Miss Tipp who initially sat on the board of directors. In 1919, after a few changes in the management, Philipp Ullmann became the exclusive proprietor. For political reasons Ullmann had to emigrate to England in 1933 like many others. From 1935 to 1945 Tipp was managed by a former Bing director, Ernst Horn. Tipp was famous for military toys. Several aeroplanes (bombers), tanks, guns and anti-aircraft guns were shown in their catalogues.

Until 1942 they still manufactured toys, but after that only war materials. Meanwhile Ullmann had founded the firm Mettoy in London and after the Second World War regained control of Tipp & Co. His son, Henry, and he were confronted with the problem of managing two toy firms. In 1971 they decided to stop Tipp's production.

# TRIX

In 1927 Stephan Bing, Oppenheimer and Erlanger took over the toy manufacturer 'Andreas Förtner and Joh. Haffner'. They started in Nuremberg by producing some tin-plate toys. The name was changed into Trix when they had a big success with a metal construction kit of the same name in about 1935. From that time they also produced small 16·5 mm gauge trains (designed by Kahn). In the same year Stephan Bing went to England, where he founded an English subsidiary company. Bassett-Lowke became the sole agent of the products of Trix Ltd.

In 1938 the German company was taken over by Ernst Völk, the man who had also taken over Distler two years earlier.

The entire factory in Nuremberg was destroyed during the Second World War, and its reconstruction was handled by Fischer and the engineers Insam and Bayer. They continued manufacturing trains and in 1971 the firm was taken over by Gama, having passed through several hands after the war.

*Uebelacker*

At the end of 1871 Leonhard Uebelacker founded a small toy firm in Nuremberg. His tin-plate collection consisted of ships, but unfortunately we know little more than this. In 1934 the name of Christian Uebelacker turned up as a manufacturer of tin-plate toys. Although there is no proof, it can be assumed there was some connection between the two toy firms.

*VEB Mechanische Spielwaren*

This firm became the successor of Lehmann in Brandenburg. When Johann Richter left in 1947, the name changed into VEB (Volkseigener Betrieb Mechanische Spielwaren).

*Wimmer*

In 1928, in Nuremburg, Heinrich Wimmer started manufacturing mechanical animals, cars, aeroplanes, etc., using clockworks from Bühler. A few years later, he decided to start manufacturing trains. After the Second World War under the influence of his son, Ernst, who joined the company in 1950, trains became the only article they produced. The founder died in 1970 and at the moment trains are still produced.

Gauge 0=1¼ in.

**Clockwork Tank Locomotive** with extra strong clockwork with superforce movement and patent regulator with brake worked from, the rail or cab **reversing gear**. Nicely japanned with nickel fittings, 5¼ in. long. Price **3/11** Post 3d.

*Advertisement from Gamage's catalogue, 1913*

# Alphabetical description of other European and American firms

Bassett-Lowke

In 1899 Wenman Bassett-Lowke formed a company in Northampton with a friend under the name of 'Bassett-Lowke & Co.'. In 1901 they started manufacturing trains and worked in mutual co-operation with Bing and Carette. The golden period of Bassett-Lowke was between 1901 and 1914. The first catalogue (a limited edition) appeared in 1901 and the last one in 1963. Some Carette, Bing and Plank products were shown in the first Bassett-Lowke catalogue. In 1901 Henry Greenly joined the firm as technical adviser.

Bing manufactured the more expensive, and Carette the simpler, train models for Bassett-Lowke who were of the opinion that only copies of real trains should be produced. Another reason was that Bassett-Lowke itself was forced to produce war material.

After the First World War the old ties with Bing were restored. As well as manufacturing in Northampton, subsidiaries were set up in Edinburgh (1922) and Manchester (1929). In 1953 the founder died and the interest in trains disappeared.

They continued production with industry-models (large models of the type driven on 'miniature railways').

In 1968 a new firm, 'Bassett-Lowke (Railways) Ltd.', was set up and an old tradition was restored.

*Bonnet*

This Parisian firm took over the production of the famous Fernand Martin Company in 1912. 'Vébé' was the trademark they used and their toy collection consisted of trucks, fire-engines, road-rollers, cranes and guns. They also manufactured mechanical tin-plate creatures such as pigeons, frogs, chickens and crocodiles. One of the Bonnet brothers, Robert, was a director of Jouets de Paris (JEP) for a time.

*Britain*

The founder of the company, William Britain, was born at the beginning of the last century. He manufactured the forerunners of the coin-operated machines we know today. One example is the sailor, standing on a box, who held a collecting plate in his left hand and the edge of his hat with his right hand. When a penny was placed in the plate, the sailor would move his arm and tip the penny. At the same time he would lift his hat, bow to the giver and recover his original position. Other examples were a walking bear and two coolies with a sedan chair and there were many others. At the turn of the century Britain and his sons decided to manufacture hollow lead toy soldiers. At the same time they changed the firm's name to Britain Ltd.

At the present time they manufacture a great variety of plastic model toys.

George Brown was born in 1830 in Bolton, Conn., U.S.A. He started work as an apprentice clockmaker. In 1856 he went into partnership with C. Goodrich in 'George W. Brown and Company' in Forestville. They manufactured clocks and also mechanical and non-mechanical tin-plate toys, such as locomotives, paddle-boats, coaches and horse-trams. After 1862 the toy-production was pushed aside by the enormous production of oil-lamps for households. In 1868 the firm was taken over by Bristol Brass and George Brown became a shareholder.

In 1869 he started another toy firm, 'Stevens and Brown' in Cromwell with the brothers J. and B. Stevens. This firm manufactured cast-iron toys as well as tin-plate toys, some of which were mechanical. In many cases Brown himself developed the mechanism. During the last years of his life, George Brown became an agent of the previously mentioned Bristol Brass Company. In 1889 he died in New York. The Stevens brothers, still possessing a second toy firm, carried on. Until about 1950 their collection consisted of mechanical money-boxes, toy pistols and cast-iron toys.

*Cardini*

This Italian firm was founded in 1922 in Omegna. Despite the fact that they were only in business for six years, Cardini were one of the leading Italian toy manufacturers. Their collection consisted of trains, ships, aeroplanes and cars. A spiral-spring clockwork was used, and their trademark on the toys was always pressed in relief. In 1928 the directors decided to stop production.

# CHAD VALLEY

This English toy firm was founded in 1897 by Joseph Johnson in Harborne, the name of the firm being taken from the river Chad which flowed near the factory. At first they only produced games and jig-saws. In 1904 on the death of the founder, the management was taken over by his son, Alfred. After the Second World War they started producing soft toys, in particular a great number of teddy-bears, in a subsidiary factory in Wellington. The tin-plate collection, especially cars and buses, was introduced during the thirties.

After 1936, Chad Valley became widely known for the introduction of the 'Ubilda' car construction kit, and after the death of Alfred Johnson, Sir James Curtis took over the management. In 1948 the 'Ubilda' construction kits were enlarged with a fire-engine, no. 10033 and a locomotive, no. 10010. The cars, racing cars, buses, etc., were made from an aluminium alloy.

In 1949 Chad Valley also produced clockwork trains in gauge o. A few years later they decided to stop tin-plate production and to use plastic instead.

*Citroën*

André Citroën was the founder of the French toy firm which produced a great many perfect scale models of cars. They were launched under the trademark 'Les jouets Citroën' and were mostly of scale 1 : 10 and sometimes 1 : 7. The factory in which these models were produced stood in Briare. During the years 1923–36 several Citroën car models were produced. In 1936 the firm C.I.J. ('Compagnie Industrielle du Jouet') took over the production. In the twenties this toy firm had already introduced some lovely clockwork cars such as an Alfa Romeo. The manufacture of the Citroën toy car models went over to J.R.D. just after the Second World War, but only a few Citroën T 45 trucks were produced by this firm.

*Faivre*

In 1860 Edmond Faivre founded a firm which specialized in mechanical tin-plate toys. Trains became the most important items, but clockwork cars were also produced. Their trademark, 'F.V.', became well known. A certain E. F. Levèvre took over the firm. In all probability production stopped at the end of the First World War.

*Gutmann*

This Parisian toy firm, Mery Gutmann, produced not only mechanical tin-plate toys, but also paint-boxes. Their 'MEMO' trademark was found on many French clockwork car models with a spiral-spring mechanism. In 1950 Gutmann introduced his crash car at the Lyons Industrial Fair. This was a car which 'crashed' on collision and became very popular in England and the United States.

*Hornby*

Hornby had an unusual start for a company. Frank Hornby, an Englishman, started creating toys for his own children. The result was the world-famous construction system, Meccano. In 1901 Frank Hornby, then thirty-eight years old, took out a patent for Meccano and until 1907 it was called 'Mechanics made easy'. In 1915 the first clockwork train was introduced to the public. The trademark on the locomotive was formed by the letters M.Ld.L.

In 1933 Hornby introduced his first 'Dinky Toy', which scored a real hit later. Frank Hornby, the founder died in the same year, but Meccano Ltd. in Liverpool went on.

In 1936 Meccano introduced a car construction kit, which consisted of a chassis with three different coach-work variations. It was followed by a set of larger scale-models.

In 1964 the firm was taken over by Lines Brothers.

*I.N.G.A.P.*

In 1919 the Italian toy firm I.N.G.A.P. was founded by Giovanni Casale, Giorgio Zattla, Pietro Zinelli, and Tullio and Anselmo Anselmi in Padua. The name was an abbreviation of 'Industria Nazionale Giocattoli Automatici Padova' and in 1921 they produced their trademark. Their first mechanical toy, a small train set, was produced about 1925. The I.N.G.A.P. toys were always driven by a coil-spring mechanism. In 1933 the following model planes were introduced: nos. 750, 464 and 476. Locomotives nos. 773 and 552 were also added to the collection. A year later I.N.G.A.P. introduced the model tanks nos. 413 and 414; the latter model had a flint mechanism in the barrel. In 1936 'Pinocchio' no. 770, 'Felix the cat' no. 765 and train sets nos. 1300/1400 in gauge 0 were the new items. Until the outbreak of the Second World War the I.N.G.A.P. collection consisted of cars, trains and some fighter planes. After the war some Alfa Romeo and Ferrari racing cars were introduced. In 1950 the production of mechanical toys ceased. In 1936 the owner, Mario Benacchio, had died and from that time the business of the largest Italian tin-plate toy firm quickly deteriorated. During the thirties, in the high-days of this establishment, the work-force consisted of about 600 staff. In 1972 I.N.G.A.P. was taken over by Eurotoys.

*Ives*

In 1868, in Plymouth, U.S.A., Edward Ryley Ives started manufacturing tin-plate figures which were set in motion by a heat source such as a candle. In 1872 his brother-in-law Blakeslee joined the firm in Bridgeport and the name changed to 'Ives, Blakeslee & Co.'. The collection of the American pioneer consisted mainly of mechanical toys driven by clockwork.

In the eighties Ives took over the Automatic Toy Works in New York. Later on they also started producing steam and clockwork trains (without rails). The first models, in gauge 0 and 1 were put on the market after 1901. Edward Ives died in 1918 and his son, Harry, took over the business. From that moment only toy trains were manufactured. Like Bing in Germany, Ives found themselves in serious financial straits after the Wall Street crash and the firm was taken over by three competitors, American Flyer, Hafner and Lionel.

*JEP* (formerly *S.I.F.*)

This Parisian firm, 'La Société Industrielle de Ferblanterie' (S.I.F.), was founded in 1899 and was well known for the manufacture of clockwork trains. After 1928 the name of the firm changed into 'Les Jouets de Paris', followed by JEP in 1932. Besides these trains they also produced other tin-plate toys, for example mechanical cars, submarines and boats. In the twenties the first electric JEP train was introduced. In 1965 they closed down their factory in the Boulevard Beaumarchais.

*Jouef*

Originally Jouef manufactured powder-boxes, cooking pans, pipes and toys. After the First World War they specialized in mechanical and electrical toys and in 1949 they introduced their race-track 'Trans-sahara'. They also produced toy planes and tractors. In 1951 Jouef showed their first mechanical train, followed in 1955 by the 'Southern Express', their first electrical version. They slowly changed over to the use of plastics for their toys.

*Joustra*

This firm was founded in 1935 by Guillaume Marx, its first small factory being in Strasbourg-Neudorf. Marx was German by birth, but had left for France in 1933. He had been one of the directors of the Bing concern. Joustra produced mechanical tinplate toys. During the Second World War production stopped, but was restarted in 1946.

*Kinsbury*
See under *Wilkins*

*Lionel*

In 1906 the young Joshua Lionel Cowen started business in New York. At first he manufactured electric tram-cars (gauge = 73 mm), but after 1920 he added trains and some other toys to his collection. In 1928 he took over a part of Ives' collection and increased production until the Second World War.

After 1945, Lionel, sometimes compared with Hornby, only manufactured trains. He was the last in the United States to offer toy trains in gauge o.

## Lines Brothers

In 1919 this English toy firm was founded in London by the Lines Brothers, Walter, Arthur and William. They had decided to go into business independently from their father, who was one of the owners of the toy firm 'G. & J. Lines'. As a trademark, they chose a triangle as a symbol of their partnership. In 1924 they installed themselves in a brand new factory in Merton, because the factories in London were too small.

In 1931 Lines took over the oldest and finest toy and model shop in the world, the 'Toy Store' in Regent Street. The pre-war Tri-ang collection consisted of such toys as pedal motor-cars, doll's prams, doll's houses, rocking horses, wooden pull-along toys and last, but not least, mechanical and non-mechanical metal toys. Lines became widely known for their 'Minic' series. These clockwork cars, built completely to scale, had disc wheels with rubber tyres, and almost every type of vehicle was represented. Other interesting products were some steam lorries and model vans with a long-running clockwork motor.

During the Second World War, Lines turned all their works over to war production. After the war a new factory was built in Merthyr Tydfil (South Wales). In 1964 Meccano Ltd. Liverpool joined the Lines Group and three well-known trademarks 'Meccano', 'Dinky Toy' and 'Hornby' were added to the toy collection. Afterwards new subsidiary companies were set up in New Zealand, Canada, Australia and South Africa.

*Martin*

In his factory on the Boulevard Ménilmontant over 100 workers were employed. Martin's creations were excellent examples of hand-painted tin-plate toys with a clockwork mechanism. Sometimes a twisted rubber band was provided as a mechanism. Between 1878 and 1912 Martin produced about 800,000 tin-plate toys. In 1912 production was taken over by Bonnet & Co. Martin died in 1919.

Until the thirties some Martin models were sold by Bonnet & Co.

*Marx*

In 1920 Louis Marx bought the well-known American toy firm 'Strauss, Man & Co.' in New York, and set up his own collection of tin-plate novelty toys. He succeeded in buying out a lot of his competitors in the thirties and in that way became the largest toy manufacturer in the world. Ninety per cent of his mass-produced toys were sold by large stores such as Woolworth

*L'Autopatte' mechanical cart no. 218 (Martin), c. 1900*

and Kresge, or by mail order. In spite of the fact that Marx Incl. did not manufacture toy trains in the first place, a number of Marx models are left. He sometimes used 'MARLINES' as a trade-mark.

After the Second World War Marx made a switch to the manufacture of plastic toys. Marx also had an English division.

*Meccano*
See under *Hornby*

*Meteor*

Some small steam-boats called Meteor K 21 and K 30 are the only examples of Dutch tin-plate toys. It is still unknown if the manufacturer was in business under the same name. These boats were sold in the thirties.

*Mettoy*

The founder of this firm was Philipp Ullmann, a former director of Tipp & Co., who fled to England in 1933. He started business

*Steamboat driven by candle power (Meteor), c. 1935*

in Northampton with the manufacture of mechanical motor-cyclists, trucks and aeroplanes.

Between 1934 and the outbreak of the Second World War they gained a certain reputation for themselves. During the war they had to produce war materials. After 1945 they continued production of the old collection for a while, but nine years later stopped; they restarted with the mass-production of their 'Corgi Toys'.

*Payà*

In 1906 the Spaniard Hermanos Payà started producing tin-plate toys in the village of Ibi, near Alicante. He manufactured his first clockwork train in 1918, and followed it with an electric copy in 1927. He also manufactured mechanical toys such as animals, aeroplanes and cars.

Payà is still one of the few manufacturers, who produces trains in gauge 0. A second factory was built in Alicante.

*Radiquet*

In 1872 Radiquet founded his company in Paris, and in 1889 went into partnership with Massiot. This French firm became well known for its superb steam boats. About 1905, however, toy production ceased.

*Rico*

In 1920 Santiago Rico Molina, Agapito Bernando Verdú and Jaime Esteve Bastand founded the Spanish toy firm Rico, in the village of Ibi. The toy collection consisted of tin-plate buses, cars and trucks, carrying from the beginning the trademark 'R.S.A.'. Rico not only produced mechanical toys, but also tin-plate kitchens and shops. Later on they added dolls to their collection and, after the Second World War, they changed over to plastic products. Recently Rico reintroduced a collection of tin-plate toys.

### Roitel

In 1880 the Frenchman Charles Roitel began to manufacture mechanical tin-plate toys. At first he made steam-engine accessories and a wind-up circus. After the turn of the century trams and cars, with clockwork mechanisms, were also produced. Around 1920 production stopped. There is confusion between the trademarks of this company and that of Rossignol as both manufacturers had the same initials.

### Rossignol

In 1868 Charles Rossignol started in Paris. After 1910 they sold trains (without rails) as well as mechanical tin-plate toys such as cars. Just after the First World War the first 'CR' trains in gauge 0 were shown to the public, and later on these were followed by electric specimens. In the twenties they offered a range of Paris buses, followed by attractive fire-engines in the thirties, all of which were driven by clockwork mechanisms.

In 1962 the company went out of business.

### Sutcliffe

In 1885 J. W. Sutcliffe founded a sheet-metal company in Horsforth, Leeds. His first toy item, produced in 1920, was a

30-cm-long battleship; it was powered by a water-circulating engine, heated by a spirit burner. Later models had a clockwork motor.

After the Second World War a number of small speed boats were introduced. The company is now run by the son of the founder and still produces about 40,000 tin-plate boats a year.

*Wells*

In 1919 the Englishman A. W. Wells, a toolmaker by profession, began manufacturing tin-plate toys on a small scale in Islington. In 1924 he moved to Walthamstow and designed a very popular clockwork train which was sold by Woolworth's. At the end of the twenties Wells produced cars, planes, fire-engines and shooting-games in addition to trains and stations. In 1932 the London firm Brimtoy Ltd., famous for its train-sets, was taken over by Wells. Following a large order by the Royal Air Force, Wells changed over to the manufacture of war materials. In 1945 the 'Wells Brimtoy Distributors Ltd.' was founded and production started in a factory in Beach Yard, Holyhead. At the end of the fifties the great flow of cheap Japanese toys increased, resulting in the closure of the factory, and the machines were moved to another factory in Holyhead. From 1946 they produced clocks and, later, household goods. After the death of the seventy-seven-year-old founder in 1965, the firm ran into financial difficulties and was taken over by C.M.T. Wells Kelo Ltd.

*Whiteley Tansley & Co.*

This small English company produced a range of tin road-vehicles under the trademark 'Whitanco'. The Liverpool firm registered their trademark in 1916.

## Wilkins

In 1880 James Wilkins founded the 'Triumph Wringer Company' in Keene, New Hampshire, U.S.A. In 1888 he obtained a patent for a cast-iron locomotive and the 'Wilkins Toy Company' came into being. The collection consisted of a fire-station, fire-engines, guns and pull-along toys. Unfortunately, the firm quickly developed financial troubles and was bought up by the youthful Harry T. Kinsbury. Until 1919 the name of the firm remained unchanged and there was a large increase in model cars. Clockwork cars, racing cars and fire-engines were a distinctive feature of this American manufacturer. In 1919 the firm changed its name to Kinsbury. At the end of the twenties, when Harry's two sons, Chester and Edward Kinsbury, were taken into the firm, the first clockwork model cars with battery-operated headlamps were produced. During the Second World War they sold their machines and thus ceased manufacturing toys.

*Advertisement from Gamage's catalogue, 1913*

# Acknowledgements

My thanks are due to:

Roel Valenteijn, Bob Leenart, Klaas and Dick Gubbels, Cor Kok, Dick Koene, Ferry Bridié, Peter Blom, J. Déwald, F. Buchwaldt sr., O. Verhagen, G. Jonker, Mary Hillier, Jac Remise, Charles Eames, Bill Holland, Monique and Jacques Milet, Raymond Spong, Mary Speaight, Dr. Lydia Bayer, Dr. Hirschmann, Wolfgang Richter, Dr. Josef Kuba, Mrs. Kammerer, Dr. Bismarck, Dr. E. Horn, F. Hosender, Mr. Leykauf, Mr. Mehler, Mr. Strecker, Mr. Winter, Mr. Steinacker, Mr. Meidenbauer, Mr. Weigelt.

Also to the toy museums of Roden and Deventer; the London Museum; State Toy Museum, Nuremberg; State Archives, Nuremberg; National Technical Museum, Prague; Association of German Toy Manufacturers; Antique Toy Collectors of America; British Toy Manufacturers Association; American Association of Museums; the Japanese Cultural Institute; Kamers van Koophandel of Amsterdam and Deventer; Gijsbers & van Loon Antiquarian Bookshop and the Public Library in Deventer, Fa. Vedeka of Amsterdam.

And to the following companies: Arnold, Britain Ltd., Bühler, C.M.T. Wells Kelo Ltd., Einfalt, Fleischmann, Jouef, Joustra, Kellermann, Kienberger, Lehmann, Mangold, Markes & Co., Märklin, Mettoy, Payà, Rico, Schrödel, Schreyer & Co., Seidel.

# Bibliography and Films

BIBLIOGRAPHY

Georg Hieronimus Bestellmeier – Magazin von verschiedenen Kunst- und anderen nützlichen Sachen (1805)
Léo Claretie – Les Jouets (1893)
Gordon Craig – Book of penny toys (1899)
Léo Claretie – Les Merveilles du Jouet à Bon Marché (1899)
Henry d'Allemagne – Histoire des Jouets (1903)
Karl Gröber – Kinderspielzeug aus alter Zeit (1928)
Hans Geist – Spielzeug. Eine bunte Fibel (1938)
Louis Hertz – Messrs. Ives of Bridgeport (1950)
Juliane Roh – Altes Spielzeug (1958)
Rabecq-Maillard – Histoire du Jouet (1962)
Leslie Diaken – World of Toys (1963)
Franz E. Braun – Das Spiel mit Stahl (1964)
Mary Hillier – Pageant of Toys (1965)
Frans Uhl – De Wereld in een kinderhand (1965)
A. Burky-Bartelink – Antiek speelgoed (1966)
Antonia Fraser – A History of Toys (1966)
Lydia Bayer – Altes Spielzueg (1967)
Jac Remise & Jean Fondain – The Golden Age of Toys (1967)
Patrick Murray – Toys (1968)
Robert Culff – The World of Toys (1969)
Louis Hertz – The Toy Collector (1969)
Claude Jeanmaire – Die grosse Spurweiten (Märklin) (1969)
Katharine McClinton – Antiques of American Childhood (1970)
Gustav Reder – Mit Uhrwerk, Dampf und Strom (1970)
J. Minns – Model Railways Engines (1970)
Edith Barenholtz – George Brown Toy Sketch Book (1971)
Gwen White – Antique Toys and their background (1971)
Claude Jeanmaire – Bing, die Modellbahnen unserer Grossväter (1972)
Carlernst Baecker und Dieter Haas – Die Anderen Nürnberger (5 volumes 1973–1976)
Gwen White – Toys, Dolls, Automata (1975)
Bossi, Marco – Autohobby (1975)
Mary Hillier – Working Toys and automata (1976)

FILMS

Charles Eames: 'Toccata for Toy trains' (1957), duration: 14 minutes
Charles Eames: 'Tops' (1969), duration: 7 minutes and 15 seconds
Jac Remise: 'Le jouet témoin de son temps' (1969), duration: 20 minutes

# Index of Trademarks

| | |
|---|---|
| GEOBRA | Georg Brandstätter, Nuremberg |
| GESCHA | Gebrüder Schmid, Nuremberg |
| G.F.N. | Gebrüder Fleischmann, Nuremberg |
| G. & K. | Gundka-Werke, Brandenburg (Greppert & Kelch) |
| G.K.N. | Georg Köhler, Nuremberg |
| G.M.C. | Gebrüder Märklin & Co., Göppingen |
| G.M. & CIE. | Gebrüder Märklin & Co., Göppingen |
| G.M. & CO. | Gebrüder Marklin & Co., Göppingen |
| GÖSO | Christian Götz & Sohn, Fürth |
| G.S.N. | Gebrüder Schmid, Nuremberg |
| H.E.N. | Hans Eberl, Nuremberg |
| HESSMOBIEL | Mattheus Hess, Nuremberg |
| H.K. | Hans Krauss, Nuremberg |
| HORNBY | Meccano Ltd., Liverpool |
| H.P. of HPAI | Hermanos Payà, Ibi |
| HUKI | Hubert Kienberger, Nuremberg |
| HUSCH | Heller & Schiller, Obersleutensdorf (Litvinov) |
| H.W.N. | Heinrich Wimmer, Nuremberg |
| I.B. & CO. | Ives, Blakeslee & Co., Bridgeport |
| I.B. & W.CO. | Ives, Blakeslee & Williams Co., Bridgeport |
| IDEAL | J. G. Schrödel, Nuremberg |
| I.M.C. | Ives Mfg. Co., Bridgeport |
| I.N.G.A.P. | Industria Nazionale Giocattoli Automatici Padova (Padua) |
| I. & W.CO. | Ives & Williams Co., Bridgeport |
| J.A.J. | Johann A. Issmayer, Nuremberg |
| J.D.N. | Johann Distler, Nuremberg |
| J.E.P. | Jouets de Paris, Paris |
| J.F. of J.F.N. | Joseph Falk, Nuremberg |
| J.H. | Jean Höfler, Fürth |
| J.H.L. | Johann Leonhard Hess, Nuremberg |
| J.K.CO. of J.K.CO.N. | Josef Kraus, Nuremberg |
| J.N.F. | Joseph Neuhierl, Fürth |
| JOUEF | Jouef, Paris |
| JOUSTRA | Jouet Strassbourg, Strasbourg |
| JOYO | Hermanos Payà, Ibi |
| J.S. | Jean Schönner, Nuremberg |
| JUMBO | Blomer & Schüler, Nuremberg |
| K.B. of K.B.N. | Karl Bub, Nuremberg |
| K.B./B.W. | Karl Bub and Bing-Werke, Nuremberg 1933 |
| K. & B.B. | Kindler & Briel, Böblingen |
| K.C.O. | Georg Kellermann & Co., Nuremberg |
| KIBRI | Kindler & Briel, Böblingen |

| | |
|---|---|
| KICO | Hubert Kienberger, Nuremberg |
| K.R.Z. | Karl Rohrseitz, Zirndorf |
| L.BROS | Lines Brothers Ltd., London |
| L.B.Z. | Lorenz Bolz, Zirndorf |
| LINEOL | Lineol A. G., Brandenburg |
| LIONEL | Lionel, New York |
| LOWKO | W. Bassett-Lowke & Co., Northampton |
| MARLINES | Louis Marx & Co., New York |
| MEMO | Mery Gutmann, Paris |
| METEOR | Meteor, Netherlands |
| METTOY | Mettoy Playthings, Northampton |
| M.F.Z. | Martin Fuchs, Zirndorf |
| M.H.N. | Mattheus Hess, Nuremberg |
| M.L.D.L. | Meccano Ltd., Liverpool |
| M.M.N. | Max Moschkowitz, Nuremberg |
| M.N.N. | Michaël Nüsslein, Nuremberg |
| M.S. | Michael Seidel, Nuremberg |
| NEW YORK FLYER | Hafner Mfg. Co., Chicago |
| ORO of OROBR. | Oro-Werke, Brandenburg |
| P.F. | Péan Frères, Paris |
| RAI | Hermanos Payà, Ibi |
| RAPIDO | Karl Arnold, Nuremberg |
| R.S.A. | Rico, Ibi |
| SCHUCO | Schreyer & Co., Nuremberg |
| S.G. | S. Günthermann, Nuremberg |
| S.I.F. | Société Industrielle de Ferblanterie, Paris |
| STOCK | Stock, Sollingen |
| T.CO. | Tipp & Co., Nuremberg |
| TECHNOFIX | Gebrüder Einfalt, Nuremberg |
| TIPPCO | Tipp & Co., Nuremberg |
| TRI-ANG | Lines Brothers Ltd., London |
| TRIX | Trix, Nuremberg |
| TRIX | Trix Ltd., London |
| UBILDA | Chad Valley, Harborne and Wellington |
| V.B. & CIE. | Victor Bonnet & Cie., Paris |
| VÉBÉ | Les Frères Bonnet, Paris |
| WHITANCO | Whiteley Tansley & Co., Liverpool |
| W.K. | Wilhelm Krauss, Nuremberg |
| W.R. | William Rissmann, Nuremberg |

174

# Index

Figures in **bold type** refer to page numbers of illustrations.